THE PSYCHOLOGY
OF EXERCISE

Why should we exercise? When should we exercise? Why don't we exercise?

The Psychology of Exercise separates fact from fiction, delving into key theories, ideas, and the impact of life stages on when, why, and how we exercise. It explores the barriers and motivators to exercise for children, teenagers, adults, and retirees as well as for those living with a chronic health condition. It shows how when we personalise activity programmes, exercise becomes a life-affirming, life-lengthening habit.

Using real-life case studies from those who work with exercisers at all levels, *The Psychology of Exercise* shows us the huge value that comes from exercising in every stage of our lives.

Dr. Josephine Perry is a Chartered Sport and Exercise Psychologist based in London, UK, and Director of Performance in Mind, a Performance Psychology Consultancy. She works with athletes, exercisers and high performers to help them achieve their goals and enjoy the process of exercise along the way.

THE PSYCHOLOGY OF EVERYTHING

People are fascinated by psychology, and what makes humans tick. Why do we think and behave the way we do? We've all met armchair psychologists claiming to have the answers, and people that ask if psychologists can tell what they're thinking. *The Psychology of Everything* is a series of books which debunk the popular myths and pseudo-science surrounding some of life's biggest questions.

The series explores the hidden psychological factors that drive us, from our subconscious desires and aversions, to our natural social instincts. Absorbing, informative, and always intriguing, each book is written by an expert in the field, examining how research-based knowledge compares with popular wisdom, and showing how psychology can truly enrich our understanding of modern life.

Applying a psychological lens to an array of topics and contemporary concerns – from sex, to fashion, to conspiracy theories – *The Psychology of Everything* will make you look at everything in a new way.

Titles in the series:

The Psychology of Grief
Richard Gross

The Psychology of Sex
Meg-John Barker

The Psychology of Dieting
Jane Ogden

The Psychology of Performance
Stewart T. Cotterill

The Psychology of Trust
Ken J. Rotenberg

The Psychology of Working Life
Toon W. Taris

The Psychology of Conspiracy Theories
Jan-Willem van Prooijen

The Psychology of Addiction
Jenny Svanberg

The Psychology of Fashion
Carolyn Mair

The Psychology of Gardening
Harriet Gross

For further information about this series please visit
www.routledgetextbooks.com/textbooks/thepsychologyofeverything/

THE PSYCHOLOGY OF EXERCISE

JOSEPHINE PERRY

Routledge
Taylor & Francis Group

LONDON AND NEW YORK

First published 2021
by Routledge
2 Park Square, Milton Park, Abingdon, Oxon OX14 4RN

and by Routledge
52 Vanderbilt Avenue, New York, NY 10017

Routledge is an imprint of the Taylor & Francis Group, an informa business

British Library Cataloguing-in-Publication Data
A catalogue record for this book is available from the British Library

Library of Congress Cataloging-in-Publication Data
A catalog record for this book has been requested

ISBN: 978-0-367-37082-4 (hbk)
ISBN: 978-0-367-37084-8 (pbk)
ISBN: 978-0-429-35261-4 (ebk)

Typeset in Joanna
by Apex CoVantage, LLC

Printed by CPI Group (UK) Ltd, Croydon CR0 4YY

CONTENTS

ABOUT THE AUTHOR

Josephine Perry, PhD, is a Chartered Sport and Exercise Psychologist in London. She is an applied practitioner working directly with athletes, stage performers and members of the public who want to use performance psychology to achieve their goals. For those focused less on sport and more on exercise, she supports them throughout their exercise journey using many of the ideas and theories detailed within this book. She is a Registered Practitioner Psychologist with the Health and Care Professions Council (HCPC), chartered with the British Psychological Society (BPS), and a member of the Association of Applied Sport Psychologists (AASP). She is also an Associate Lecturer at the Open University.

Perry writes extensively. She has written the book *Performing under Pressure: Strategies for Sporting Success* and hundreds of features for magazines such as *Cycling Weekly*, *Men's Fitness*, *Runners World*, *Athletics Weekly* and *Golf World*. She is regularly asked to speak as an expert on news and documentary programmes and works closely with journalists to offer advice and guidance on how to use sport and exercise psychology to improve performance and enjoyment of exercise.

ACKNOWLEDGEMENTS

I would like to thank the team at Routledge for giving me this opportunity to explore and explain such an important area and for all their support along the way.

It has been a real privilege to work in this area and to be able to describe to the world why the psychology of exercise is so important. I am particularly grateful for those who have taken the time to illuminate how they work with different groups of people to enhance their exercise levels, build enjoyment and put in place activities which ensure long-term adherence. This includes Hannah Corne and the Mini Mermaids team, Diana Thesee and the girls at Skates Dagenham, Professor Sally Wyke and the men who have thrived on the FFIT programme, Eddie Brocklesby and the Silverfit members, Lucy Gossage and Gemma Hilier-Moses who run 5k Your Way for those living with cancer, and Marianne who so generously and openly talked about her exercise addiction.

My family has been very patient and understanding when I spend yet another day locked in the office researching and writing, so thank you to Paul and Hattie. My extended family have forgiven me for many missed coffee dates, so also thanks to Jenny, James and Henry.

Finally, and most importantly, I would like to thank all those I have supported on their sport or exercise journeys over the years. I am sure I learn more from the athletes and exercisers I work with than they will ever learn from me, and I am eternally grateful.

INTRODUCTION

If a pharmaceutical company developed a new product which would increase muscular and cardiorespiratory fitness, improve bone and functional health, reduce the risk of hypertension, coronary heart disease, stroke, diabetes, cancer, anxiety and depression, lower the likelihood of falls and fractures, boost mood and quality of life and cut down on loneliness, their share price would skyrocket. They would be able to charge a fortune and still save health systems money.

There is such a product. But it isn't a pill. It is an activity. A physical activity, in fact: exercise. Exercise has tremendous powers which, when taken regularly and with the right intensity, can make a huge difference to our mental and physical health.

The problem is that exercise isn't as easy as popping a pill. Exercise is more than just physical activity. It is purpose-driven movement aiming to improve our fitness and so requires physical effort, occasional discomfort and time to be executed well. And to even get to that point there are a whole host of psychological, logistical, environmental, sociological and sometimes physical barriers to overcome. As a result of these barriers, up to 71% of adults in some parts of the world (Hallal et al., 2012) are not active enough, resulting in insufficient physical activity being one of the leading risk factors of global mortality. As inactivity levels rise, the risks continue to grow, with those who are insufficiently active increasing their risk of death by up to 30% (WHO, 2018b). There is also a significant financial burden of this inactivity with conservative estimates putting the cost on health care systems at $53.8 billion worldwide (Ding et al., 2016).

Behind these huge global figures sit individuals. Their years are cut short, their wellbeing is harmed and their quality of life is limited. The harm they suffer makes the case for the role of exercise, in every stage of our lives, to be magnified. This book attempts to begin that magnification. We will address the psychological and cognitive benefits of exercising, the barriers and facilitators towards exercise and evidence-based programmes which have been shown to be effective in increasing how active we are. We break these all down via life stages, so the knowledge delivered is tailorable for individual audiences.

From both a physical and mental perspective it is vital we understand the psychology behind exercise. When we become self-aware of our exercise behaviours, we can reflect on the barriers we confront, embrace the facilitators and motivators we see and find ways to learn from others so we can successfully embed exercise within our lives. The evidence, research and best practice held within these pages should help you to do that, either for yourself or others.

Our journey through these pages should highlight how exercise improves our behaviours, our mental health and our cognitive performance throughout each stage of life. We will consider the barriers and facilitators that impact how much exercise we do, and we will look at those people who may influence us. By understanding the relative importance of the different influences on exercise, we can create a library of knowledge from which to direct and shape strategies on which to focus and evidence-based programmes which work. Through this we will offer best practice for designing programmes or interventions which get us exercising and stay engaged with it. We will also consider some interventions that have worked really well, offering great examples of programmes that are exercise based, effective and have been life-changing for all those involved.

Initially, *The Psychology of Exercise* will introduce you to the key theories, ideas and models of exercise psychology. Research shows that physical activity interventions designed using theoretically driven approaches are most effective (Kahn et al., 2002), so initially, in Chapter 1, we will look to understand the main theories and models of exercise psychology. Understanding the motives that influence physical activity participation is critical for developing interventions to promote higher levels of involvement. Within these we should be able to note the individual, social, environmental and societal influences on exercise engagement and consider how behavioural strategies and support can improve adherence to exercise programmes. Initiation of exercise is underpinned by complex decision-making and goal-setting processes, and so we need a good grasp of these. After this, each chapter will tackle a different life stage, focusing right across our life cycle and addressing the psychology of exercise from childhood through retirement and for those with specific health conditions.

When we consider the role of the psychology of exercise for children in Chapter 2, we will look at the role of schools in supporting and developing exercise habits and activities and address the impact of young onset obesity on psychological development of healthy lifestyle attitudes. We now know that the decline in physical activity begins at age seven (Farooq et al., 2018), so it is essential we help children develop a habit for exercising while young.

As those children move into adolescence, Chapter 3 considers the importance, barriers and facilitators of exercise in teenagers. We will look at why so many young people drop out of exercise in their teens, the barriers they face and what needs to be included within an intervention to engage and motivate them to continue or get back into participation.

As we hit adulthood (Chapter 4), we will look at the benefits that being physically active brings when you are fully independent and handling the pressures that come with grown-up life. The barriers that we face when living a more responsible lifestyle, however, are high, particularly around caring for both children and parents. As we can see that parents' exercise levels play a huge influence on their children's levels of physical activity, finding positive and effective programmes to support people is vital.

In Chapter 5 we consider how retirees see exercise. The specific barriers and facilitators change significantly when the pressures of work have left but the physical, economic and psychological restrictions of older age have arrived. We will look at the fears around falls and caring responsibilities but also the joy that exercise brings to develop social engagements and reduce loneliness.

Throughout our lives, when we are in good health, the benefits of exercise are easy to spot, the barriers can be confronted and the facilitators utilised. When we develop a chronic health condition, this becomes excessively harder. In Chapter 6 we see the huge psychological benefits of physical activity when someone is facing type 2 diabetes, depression, asthma, cardiovascular disease or cancer but also how the diseases themselves negatively impact on our ability or willingness to exercise. We set out evidence-based intervention programmes which could support those facing these types of health conditions.

Finally, while every other chapter has considered how most individuals can be supported to complete more exercise, Chapter 7 considers how to support those who are doing too much –those with exercise addiction. We will look at why they may do this, the harm it can cause their bodies and the conflict it can bring in their relationships. We will address the routes that can be taken to reduce these risks.

In breaking down the psychology of exercise into these distinct stages of life, it is hoped that the evidence given and interventions discussed will provide valuable insight to help ourselves and others enjoy the mental and physical benefits of being active. When we understand the psychology of exercise, we can make better decisions and live healthier, more enjoyable lives.

1

THEORIES AND MODELS OF EXERCISE PSYCHOLOGY

There are 7.7 billion people on the planet, and each of us is unique. No two people will enjoy exactly the same type of exercise, for the same reason, having overcome the same barriers or been motivated by the same passions. We each have different levels of self-efficacy and intention to exercise and support mechanisms around us. This means the ideal way to get someone motivated to exercise, to overcome each of the barriers in their way and to stick to their exercise long term, is to provide personalised support from an expert who can shape and tailor everything effectively. However, with the huge numbers of people not yet exercising to the levels needed for good physical and mental health, some shortcuts are needed, and theories and models of exercise psychology can help with that. When we study and try to understand exactly what is happening when someone is engaged (or not) in exercise, we can use these theories and models as a basis for interventions which are more effective for more people and that will have a much longer-lasting impact.

The theories that have been developed can be categorised into five areas: self-regulation and motivation, social cognitive, stage based, belief and body image. Within each area the key theories which are regularly used within exercise psychology are discussed. There are also a few more interconnected theories which we will consider.

SELF-REGULATION AND MOTIVATIONAL MODELS

Self-regulation and motivational frameworks have been developed to help us understand what inspires and influences us to take up and continue with physical activities. They highlight the key aspects of the processes which help us to become motivated and then regulate our behaviours. These will include feedback processes and emotional responses which can guide goal pursuit and progress. They also include goals which provide the cognitive links between motivations and specific behaviours. Tactics (such as self-monitoring, goal setting, reinforcement, and self-corrective actions) that are often found in models like this have been used successfully and with long-lasting effects.

SELF-DETERMINATION THEORY (DECI & RYAN, 2000)

One of the most well-used motivational theories is the Self-Determination Theory (SDT). The theory links personality, human motivation and optimal functioning, offering an insight as to why we adopt and maintain certain behaviours. It helps us consider the inherent and social-contextual conditions that influence how we think, feel and behave and suggests we will experience more self-determined forms of motivation when we experience greater feelings of autonomy (where we feel able to take control of our own destiny and behaviours), relatedness (our need to feel connected to our social surroundings and cared for by the people in them) and competence (our feelings of efficacy to perform or display our exercise skills to a high level). It has been used extensively to understand exercise and physical activity participation.

The theory suggests that if we satisfy these three psychological needs of autonomy, competence and relatedness when we exercise, we will achieve optimal motivation, increased exercise engagement and positive wellbeing. When our three needs are frustrated, our motivation suffers.

In developing SDT, Deci and Ryan distinguished between different types of motivation based on the reasons or goals that give rise to the action. They suggest there are three types of motivation sitting on a continuum with non-self-determined (amotivated) through extrinsically motivated to self-determined (intrinsically motivated). When we have no interest in exercise, we will be considered amotivated and are unlikely to do very much physical activity.

When we are starting our exercise journey, we will often be extrinsically motivated, doing the exercise because it leads to a separate outcome (such as getting a reward or praise). In this mode we might be exercising because we feel guilty if we don't, and while this works for a while, there is no self-determination and so no true personal endorsement. Over time this means we either stop or, more hopefully, we begin to internalise some of that motivation to exercise, and we move into a maintenance stage where we are now exercising with some intrinsic motivation.

When we feel competent and able to perform the skill or exercise we want to and have a choice over what we are doing, then our intrinsic motivation will be highest and the more likely we are to exercise. Over time, as we internalise and integrate exercise into our lives, we exercise because it matches our sense of self, and this gives us autonomous motivation. Here we spend the time and effort doing it purely for the pleasure of the movement, feelings or enjoyment. But even when we feel competent, if we don't feel we have any choice about performing that exercise or skill, then intrinsic motivation is likely to fall. This state, when we have competence and relatedness but no autonomy, is known as controlled motivation. Here we have fewer self-determined reasons for our goals, and they are filtered through self-imposed sanctions such as guilt, shame or pride or through external regulation where behaviours are focused on achieving externally based rewards. When none of our needs are satisfied, it is unlikely we will willingly exercise.

SELF-REGULATION FOR CHRONIC DISEASE CONTROL (CLARK, GONG & KACIROTI, 2001)

The self-regulation for chronic disease control model can be a helpful framework for those working with people suffering from chronic conditions (Chapter 6) who are trying to increase their exercise levels. The model incorporates principles from the social cognitive theory (see the next section) to show the cognitive and behavioural processes involved in trying to achieve health-related goals. Within the model the individual will observe their current exercise behaviours, reflect on what this is telling them, try to make changes, and then reflect again on their cognitive reactions to these behavioural change attempts. It brings out the importance of self-awareness in our exercise journey and suggests that the reflection process influences our subsequent behaviour.

BROADEN AND BUILD THEORY (FREDRICKSON, 2004)

The Broaden and Build Theory focuses on positive emotions. It describes how these positive emotions (such as joy, interest, contentment and love) move us away from the negative automatic and immediate responses we often have (often responding to threat or fear) and instead broaden our mindset. This can help us have a wider attention span (focusing on the good stuff) and process the things around us more positively. With this more positive mindset, we start to build our psychological resources which help us develop new skills or supportive relationships, the polar opposite of the narrowed mindset focus which comes from our threat responses. For exercise it means instead of trying to overcome the barriers we might have around threat within exercise, such as embarrassment of being seen in tight clothing or fear of failing to become competent in new skills, we focus on what we enjoy about the exercise and where it could take us. The theory suggests that once the positive mindset has been developed, our resilience and wellbeing improve. When tested with those with health conditions, self-awareness increases, resulting in wider behavioural repertoires, so they have more mental resources to cope and are able to improve their quality of life.

SOCIAL COGNITIVE MODELS AND THEORIES

Social cognitive models of health behaviour suggest that individual differences in our exercise behaviours are influenced by our attitudes and beliefs towards exercise. If we believe that the advantages of exercising outweigh the disadvantages, we will evaluate exercise as important to us and so have a more positive attitude towards it and be more likely to do it.

The stronger an individual's beliefs and values are around a sport, then the more time they have been found to spend doing it (Eccles & Harold, 1991). A similar relationship has been found between parents' beliefs and their children's level of activity (Fredricks & Eccles, 2005). This could either be that they think highly of sport so spend a lot of time doing it, or they spend a lot of time doing it so think higher of sport. Either way, these models help us to understand the links between beliefs and behaviours.

When these social cognitive models are taken out into society and used with potential exercisers, they can provide a framework to help us understand how environmental and contextual cues (such as social support or norms from peers and family), cognitions (knowledge of the exercise, risk awareness or commitment required) and intrapersonal skills (such as self-efficacy or self-regulation strategies) lead us towards our exercise beliefs, leading us to exercise in the way we do. When we are aware of the variables that help us develop our beliefs, we know better what to consider when creating exercise programmes.

EXPECTANCY-VALUE MODEL (PARSONS, ADLER, FUTTERMAN, ET AL., 1983)

The expectancy-value model assumes that our expectancies (our beliefs around our ability or whether we are likely to succeed) and task values (the attainment, intrinsic, utility and cost values that are needed to invest) affect both what exercise we decide to do and the effort and persistence we put into it. Using this algorithm, we can break the model down to understand why someone is exercising. If we took a female who has completed a couch to 5k programme and now runs regularly, the expectancy might be her belief that she is good at running. The values would be the importance she gives to being a decent runner (attainment), her enjoyment of running (intrinsic), the goals she achieves through her running (utility) and how tired it makes her (cost). The theory suggests it is these beliefs and values which impact whether she chooses to run or not, and as this example shows, it can be helpful to understand our choices around exercise and see where we may need to step in to boost motivation.

The model is suggesting that socialisation is an active social process in which values and norms are transmitted and that this will impact whether someone is likely to exercise. Here the socialising agents (such as teachers and parents for children, or peers and family for adults) become important as their values and expectations would have an influence on whether they start to exercise and are likely to continue. These values and expectations are built into an expectancy-value framework where our beliefs around our abilities and our expectations work alongside each other to influence our choices, effort levels and persistence.

SOCIAL COGNITIVE THEORY (BANDURA, 1989)

Social Cognitive Theory proposed that our behaviours are the result of dynamic and reciprocal interactions between personal, behavioural and environmental factors. It suggests we can't follow a process of X causes Y which impacts Z because relationships are too complex and too interactive. As a result, this theory is not really designed to help predict behaviour but instead to guide us through some grounding principles which can be used to develop behaviour change interventions. In doing so it suggests that we acquire skills and develop new behaviours because we see successful ones working for ourselves and for others. What we observe develops expectations about what should be possible, thus improving our self-efficacy and understanding of the positive or negative consequences of our behaviours.

SOCIAL COMPARISON THEORY (FESTINGER, 1954)

When we compare and evaluate ourselves against others, we allow our own social and personal worth to be based on how we rank ourselves against other people. It can initially occur as a way of fostering self-improvement, motivation or to develop a more positive self-image. Those doing it regularly, social comparison theory suggests, may end up feeling deep dissatisfaction, guilt or remorse and start to behave destructively. The judgemental nature of the evaluations will not only be riddled with bias but fails to take into account the myriad of elements which impact on our own exercise journey. Extracting yourself from this type of thinking requires a huge amount of work and a lot of emotional control for people to develop and stick to their own goals and value systems around exercise.

When social comparison has been used within exercise interventions, it has sometimes been used to place overweight people alongside normal weight people to highlight each group's strengths (for example, someone who is overweight might see they are better at resistance exercises, which could increase their self-worth). However, there are so many elements to social comparison that many researchers feel it is actually likely to highlight negative differences, and this could harm autonomous motivation.

PROBLEM-BEHAVIOUR THEORY (JESSOR & JESSOR, 1977)

Problem-behaviour theory looks at both the risk and protective factors regulating how we behave and transgress against norms. It was developed for problem behaviours and has been adapted for use with health behaviours. The idea is that most health-enhancing behaviours (healthy eating habits, regular exercise, adequate sleep, dental care and safety practices) are encouraged and supported by agents and institutions (such as family or school), so we can look for variables explicitly used to account for the adherence or transgression of conventional norms in order to see if health behaviours are followed. The difficulty with using this model as a basis to increase exercise adherence is that in some environments the social norm is inactivity. In pushing exercise, we would need to be actively promoting transgression. Where exercise is the norm though, it can be used, at least in the initial stages, to get someone started on an exercise journey.

STEREOTYPE EMBODIMENT THEORY (LEVY, 2009)

Stereotypes are the shared beliefs we have about the behaviours and characteristics of a group of people with something in common. It has been proposed that stereotypes can come to reality when they are assimilated from the culture and that this process can influence how we function and how we consider our health. This assimilation can be particularly strong and unhelpful with vulnerable communities such as those with a health condition. The stereotype embodiment theory suggests that once these stereotypes have been assimilated, they can become a barrier to exercise engagement as the populations believe the stereotype suggesting they have low exercise capabilities. When we recognise this, we can look at each group and try to unselect the stereotypes which are focused on exercise capability to block internalisation of these beliefs, ensuring they no longer stay a barrier to exercise.

STAGE-BASED MODELS

A number of models flow from the idea that the process of behaviour change is neither linear nor one-dimensional; instead the process of becoming someone who exercises is made up of a number of stages from initial response, continued response, maintenance and, hopefully, habit.

Most stage models tend to see the initial response as the period when a person's self-efficacy to try and start exercise and their motivation for doing so is really important. Ideally their self-efficacy will increase once the initial stage is complete as they have had an opportunity to become more competent in the required movements and master the skills of their chosen exercise. This helps them stick with it even when they face barriers or reduced motivation along the way. As someone transitions into the maintenance phase, most models suggest that the focus has moved away from whether someone is physically able to do the exercise and is more on how much they are valuing the exercise and recognising any benefits from it. Once they are in the habit phase, a self-sustaining pattern of behaviour should be in place, and it is only when large barriers or crises occur (such as a health condition or job loss) that their habitual intentions to exercise may be thwarted. Within a stages model, elements like self-efficacy, motivation and barriers may fluctuate to their importance or impact during different periods.

TRANSTHEORETICAL MODEL (PROCHASKA & DICLEMENTE, 1983)

To understand the mechanisms involved in the process of behavioural change, the transtheoretical model has become one of the most commonly used models and is widely used in intervention programmes. Stemming from addiction studies, it assumes that behavioural change is a dynamic, non-continuous process and incorporates a host of theories each contributing to the explanation of the processes of intentional behavioural changes. Five elements are incorporated: stages of change, decisional balance, temptation, self-efficacy and processes of change. Within these it recognises elements from belief models and from self-regulation and motivation models. When the transtheoretical model has been applied, it has been found to explain a significant percentage of decision-making around exercise intention.

The theory begins with an assumption that behavioural change takes place in six discrete stages based on our readiness to change: pre-contemplation (not intending to change in the next six months), contemplation (intending to change in the next six months), preparation (intending to change during the next month), action (already started to change), maintenance (been engaged in exercise for over six months) and termination. The theory suggests the process is cyclical, and while some people remain in the same stage for a while, others will progress to a higher stage or drop to a lower stage over time.

The next dimension, decisional balance, is a multidimensional set of values perceived as the advantages and disadvantages that come with behavioural change. We then have temptation, which describes urges to engage in a specific habit in the midst of difficult situations. For exercise this will cover when we are likely to disengage and become inactive and what could prompt this. Being aware of this can help us to put in place coping strategies. Our self-efficacy is also an important dimension in this model as our judgement of our capability to organise and execute the required course of action to perform exercise will be based upon how confident we are to exercise and achieve our exercise goals.

Finally, the transtheoretical model doesn't just look at why and when people change but also how. The last dimension covers the process of change strategies used to look at our experiences and environment, including both cognitive (what we are thinking) and behavioural (what we are doing) elements. The cognitive processes might involve: consciousness-raising (where we seek new information to gain understanding and feedback about exercise), dramatic relief (our emotions about exercise), self-re-evaluation (our personal perspective of ourselves as an exerciser), environmental re-evaluation (how our lack of exercise is impacting on us physically and socially) or social liberation (our awareness of how exercising could lead to a healthier lifestyle). Alongside this our behavioural processes, such as counterconditioning (when we substitute new behaviours such as exercise for the problem behaviour such as inactivity), helping relationships (getting support), reinforcement management (changing the contingencies that maintain our inactivity), self-liberation (choice and commitment to start exercising) and stimulus control (control of situations that trigger our inactivity), are all important too.

The transtheoretical model is really practical as once we understand the features of each of the stages of change in exercise participation and we can see the motivations associated with each stage and transition, then we should be able to offer effective programmes to people at each stage to increase their exercise levels.

HEALTH ACTION PROCESS APPROACH MODEL (SCHWARZER, 2008)

A simpler stages of change approach is the Health Action Process Approach (HAPA). Just as the transtheoretical model uses stages of change to explain the initiation and maintenance of health behaviours, this approach does, too, but breaks them down into only three stages. In exercise these groups would be described as 'pre-intenders' (in a motivational phase where they have yet to make plans to exercise), 'intenders' (where they are in a volitional phase setting up processes for transforming their intentions into behaviour) and 'actors' (who have started exercising). The model is regularly revised as it is tested against a number of health behaviours and with different groups of people.

When applied within intervention activities, the HAPA can be used to change potentially health-damaging behaviours and replace them with healthier ones as it describes a number of motivational determinants that are important for us to formulate our intention to initiate, develop or maintain exercise. The process shows outcome expectancies, task self-efficacy (whether we feel we can do it), our risk perception, our barriers and resources all leading to the initial intention being formed. To bring this to life we can consider an older person who is currently inactive. The HAPA might bring to the fore how they might make their decision based on their perception of risk around it (e.g. I am at risk of type 2 diabetes), certain outcome expectations (e.g. exercise will help me control my weight better) and what is known as 'distinct action self-efficacy' (where we believe we are able to do the specific thing required – (e.g. I can do exercise). When these are in place, the model says this person should develop an intention to exercise regularly.

To turn intentions into actions the HAPA suggests we do 'action planning' where we specify when, where and how we want to implement the behaviour. This planning is seen to increase our commitment and the likelihood of the exercise occurring. As plans can easily hit roadblocks (it is raining or childcare plans fall through), there is a second element called 'coping planning' so strategies are put in place to overcome these potential barriers, which helps us stick to our exercise intention.

BELIEF MODELS

Belief models focus internally. They look at our perception of ourselves, the exercise and the environment we are putting ourselves into before we decide whether are capable or willing to engage with exercise.

SELF-EFFICACY THEORY (BANDURA, 1997)

A number of exercise psychology theories include constructs or mechanisms which seem to be vital to the success of any exercise interventions or programmes. One of the most important and regularly required is the self-efficacy theory. Self-efficacy is the mechanism where we ask ourselves (subconsciously) how well we are likely to be able to carry out the required action. It is our confidence in our abilities to achieve something in spite of the obstacles we may face. The higher our self-efficacy, the higher our performance should be – whether that is in a specific sport or in spending more time exercising. It has been found that those with higher self-efficacy report significantly better wellbeing and less distress during exercise, are less likely to be influenced by barriers and will be more likely to enjoy it (Dishman et al., 2005).

According to self-efficacy theory, our behaviour is determined by our self-efficacy and in our outcome expectations (what we feel will be the result of doing the behaviour). The stronger our self-efficacy and the higher our outcome expectations are around exercise the more likely we are to exercise. Studies suggest that the self-efficacy element is a stronger determinant of our exercise levels than our outcome expectations.

Bandura has demonstrated that self-efficacy beliefs can shape the exercise choices we make, how much effort we put in, how long we persevere for and how we feel about that exercise, predicting how persistent we are, how strong we are at trying to overcome our barriers and how intense our efforts might be. Further studies have found self-efficacy was the only variable to accurately predict the maintenance of any exercise programme (McAuley, Lox, & Duncan, 1993). This suggests measuring someone's self-efficacy and putting in place techniques to increase it can be really beneficial within intervention programmes. This was demonstrated when researchers assigned sedentary adults to an exercise programme. They found both short- and long-term exercise sessions resulted in an increase in self-efficacy (McAuley, Shaffer, & Rudolph, 1995), and this self-efficacy led to a reduction in physique anxiety and helped the individuals feel better able to do more exercise. The impact is circular, however, and this is key when we consider the use of self-efficacy within interventions. When we do something and are successful, it boosts our self-efficacy, which means we are more likely to continue the behaviour. When we fail at something, we undermine our self-efficacy and it falls. Therefore, when we incorporate ways to build self-efficacy, we may also need to find ways to protect against significant failure early in the exercise journey so it can be built up enough to be resilient against setbacks.

THEORY OF PLANNED BEHAVIOUR (AJZEN 1991)

The Theory of Planned Behaviour suggests that our attitude towards exercise, our beliefs around the expected benefit or harm we will get, our potential enjoyment, how difficult we anticipate it will be and how we feel others will view us will lead to an intention, and this intention will then lead to a behaviour being performed. It was developed from the Theory of Reasoned Action (Fishbein & Ajzen, 1975), which said that our attitude towards exercise and the subjective norms (such as the social pressures we are subject to) will lead to a behavioural intention, and this intention leads to a behaviour (doing more exercise). Studies of health behaviours have found that the theory of planned behaviour actually works better as a predictor of exercise behaviour, with one meta-analysis suggesting it could explain about 40% of the variance in exercise intention and around 30% of exercise behaviour in a number of different populations.

This success comes from the theory's approach that our attitude towards exercise can come from either our affective attitudes (such as the enjoyment it will give us) or our instrumental attitudes (such as how much benefit it will bring us). Studies suggest our affective attitudes are far better predictors of intention. The societal pressure we feel to exercise can include both injunctive (others think I should exercise) and descriptive (we all exercise). Similar to Bandura's self-efficacy concept our perceived behavioural control will determine both our intention and our behaviour shaping our perception of how easy or difficult we will find exercise.

The theory has been criticised by those who say social behaviour is not driven by explicit attitudes but by implicit ones and that the theory is not sensitive enough to pick up on these. There are also criticisms suggesting that the intention – action relationship is too simplistic, as there is a clear gap between what we intend and what we actually do. On one side some people intend to exercise but don't, and on the other some will exercise without positive exercise intention or deliberation, especially if they have developed exercise as a habit. The current position is that cognitive deliberation (the thoughts about behavioural control and the generation of our intentions) will guide behaviour when our habit strength is low, but this need for the cognitive deliberation reduces when habit strength is high.

When planning interventions using the Theory of Planned Behaviour, we can clearly identify the three constructs to take into account. For example, someone currently inactive would use their attitude (e.g. doing more exercise will make me healthier), the subjective norm (all my friends exercise) and perceived behavioural control (if I start by walking more, I will be able to achieve this) to develop an intervention which would use walking with friends to improve their fitness.

BODY IMAGE MODELS

Body image models may be too simplistic to explain in their entirety why we do or do not exercise, but they do play a part in understanding some motivations and barriers. The Exercise and Self-Esteem model (Sonstroem & Morgan, 1989) aims to show that there are positive emotional and psychological benefits to exercise. It outlines how exercise and exercise interventions may affect physical self-perceptions, thus leading to enhanced overall self-esteem through increased physical self-efficacy. This model has been used as a framework for describing the exercise-self-relationship. Researchers studying the link between physical activity and self-esteem in 12-year-old children in schools in Canada found a negative relationship between physical activity and body mass index and a positive one between physical activity and self-esteem (Tremblay, Inman, & Willms, 2000). When a researcher considered the exercise and self-esteem model in middle-aged women over the course of two years, they found that physical activity, self-efficacy and a reduced body mass index were linked to improved self-perceptions in relation to physical attractiveness and physical condition (Elavsky, 2010).

Another body image model, Objectification Theory (Fredrickson & Roberts, 1997), follows the central idea that the repeated experience of being treated as an object to be looked at and evaluated gradually socialises women and girls to self-objectify and internalise the observer's perspective of their body. This self-objectification develops into self-consciousness to a point where we are continually monitoring our appearance. This process can lead to increased exercise, but rather than being in a positive way, it will see increased levels of body shame and appearance anxiety, which can increase the risk of eating disorders and mental health issues.

INTERCONNECTED THEORIES

Finally, there are a few theories which aim to cut across the other models to facilitate a wider range of concepts and elements influencing our intentions, motivations and actions regarding exercise.

Many of the theories and models in this chapter highlight the huge number of individual differences which influence our exercise behaviour. The elements identified are often complex and cut across a number of factors including physiological, behavioural, cognitive, social and genetic. This has led some to suggest a Transdisciplinary Framework (Bryan et al., 2011) to consider who is likely to exercise and why. The framework is complex but shows the interrelatedness of genetic factors influencing both an individual's physiological responses to exercise (such as our temperature regulation) and our more subjective experience (such as our perceived levels of exertion). It shows how motivation influences exercise behaviour, which then influences the physiological responses to exercise, which will impact our affective responses to exercise, again leading to increased motivation to exercise. The framework suggests that our ability to adapt to and cope with exercise both physiologically and psychologically will determine whether we will respond to an intervention, and if we understand all these elements better, we will be able to more effectively design and implement interventions which work.

Similarly, the Theoretical Domains Framework (Michie et al., 2005) identifies the factors which can be modified within exercise interventions. The framework takes into account 14 domains (knowledge; skills; memory, attention and decision processes; behavioural regulation; social/professional role and identity; beliefs about capabilities; optimism; beliefs about consequences; intentions; goals; reinforcement; emotion; environmental context and resources; and social influences), making it a really useful way for us to understand barriers and facilitators related to health and exercise behaviour. This means before interventions are designed, a really wide range of influences can be considered so we create a more engaging and enticing environment for exercise to take place.

The variety of models and theories shown here highlights that no one route has been found to successfully predict to a very high level how much exercise we will do, which exercise behaviours we will show or what elements can help or hinder our journey into developing an exercise identity. But those offered should provide enough food for thought to allow us to have a thorough basis from which to work with either ourselves or others when we want to develop motivation, predict barriers, utilise facilitators and create exercise programmes or interventions which have the greatest chance of working.

2

THE PSYCHOLOGY OF
EXERCISE IN CHILDREN

We often have an image of children being incredibly active, spending as much time as they can outside and rarely sitting still, exhausted parents trailing along behind them trying to keep up. We visualise them before school, in breaks and at lunchtime chasing each other around playgrounds and then heading off to after-school physical activities. This is not the reality.

While the World Health Organisation recommends children do 60 minutes of moderate to vigorous physical activity a day, only 47% of children actually meet this target in England and only 25% in the US. Observations of really young children (two to five years old) have found they sit or stand still for about 60% of the time and are only really active for about 11% of the time. This equates to seven minutes of movement an hour (Pate, Pfeiffer, Trost, Ziegler, & Dowda, 2004), enough to fulfil WHO requirements but far less than we would imagine and for which we would certainly hope.

A child who is active when young is more likely to maintain an exercise habit for life. This lifelong habit will bring a huge number of benefits, not only physically but mentally, socially and developmentally. The physical health benefits are plentiful and covered extensively elsewhere, but there are also psychological benefits for children not only around improved cognitive function during a key time in their brain's development but also in improving mental health, mood and self-esteem.

COGNITIVE DEVELOPMENT BENEFITS

Cognition covers many different aspects of our mental functioning, such as our thought processing, memory, attention, concentration and creativity. These mental abilities begin to develop in early childhood, and as children go through school, they are significantly enhanced. Exercise has been found to positively impact cognition in children, even in those as young as four. There are a number of theories as to why. Some suggest it is the impact of cardiovascular fitness, others that it is related to higher motor coordination abilities and others still that it is due to the children engaging in goal-directed, effortful mental involvement. More simply it could be that the exercise elevates blood flow in the brain, improving cognitive functioning or that it speeds up the release of key neurotransmitters (chemicals in our brain which help send messages), elevating our arousal level and enhancing our cognitive performance.

One specific element of cognition which is improved due to exercise is executive functioning. Executive functions are the higher-level cognitive processes that manage other more basic cognitive functions. They allow us to address novel events, override habitual or automatic actions and respond properly to the environment or external context. They include planning, self-regulation, working memory (a type of short-term memory), initiation (the prompt to start something), inhibition (control over our responses) and cognitive flexibility (the ability to quickly switch between tasks). They are all highly relevant in preadolescent children as they are crucial for adaptive behaviour and development. Small changes in executive function can create large changes in behaviour, emotional regulation and social interactions, all essential to develop as a young child.

The behavioural element is particularly interesting as physical activity has been found to significantly improve the way children behave in their social environment, allowing them to co-operate better, decrease aggressiveness, take more responsibility and reduce antisocial behaviour. These behavioural regulation elements all increase a child's ability to perform in an academic environment. It has even been tested to see if incorporating exercise into the lives of those with disorders characterised by executive function deficits such as ADHD could have benefits, and there have been some promising positive outcomes.

Another area of executive function is attention, the ability to appropriately allocate processing resources to relevant stimuli. When Schmidt and colleagues (2015) studied the impact of an acute bout of coordinative exercise on the attention of 90 primary school children, they found that children's attentional performance increased through the physical education lesson for up to 90 minutes after they finished. This is really positive from an educational aspect as it means there could be benefits in the classroom after taking physical activity breaks.

Overall, the largest effects of acute bouts of physical activity occur 11–20 minutes after exercise and last only a brief time after exercise is stopped. A study of 171 overweight children aged 7–11 found that there was a dose response effect, so completing 40 minutes would have a bigger impact than doing just 20 minutes (Davis et al., 2011).

Finally, as part of our executive function, there is our working memory. There have been a large number of studies that suggest a link between exercise and working memory. Interestingly, working memory capacity is the only executive function to benefit from long-term exercise, which means it can be crucial for children studying as the benefits last long after the exercise session has ended, and benefits have been found from both motor and cardiovascular exercise. There is a strong predictive ability of working memory for academic achievement, and studies looking at academic achievement and exercise have also shown a positive link.

MENTAL HEALTH, MOOD AND SELF-ESTEEM BENEFITS

From a mental health perspective, the benefits of exercise for children include improving self-esteem and self-perception and reducing depression, tension and anxiety.

The dose response effect seen on executive function is also evident in reducing depression. The more exercise children do, the fewer depressive symptoms they experience. Mood has also been found to be improved by exercise. When nine- and ten-year olds were asked to do a fun run and play with a ball it was noted they significantly increased their positive moods and significantly decreased their negative moods (Williamson, Dewey, & Steinberg, 2001).

Our overall mental health can be improved by having higher self-esteem, and exercise can certainly contribute towards this. Our self-esteem comes from the discrepancy between how we wish we were and how we actually are, so the closer we perceive we actually are to how we would like to be, the higher our self-esteem. Self-esteem is higher with regular involvement in sport or exercise as high motor competence, good cardiovascular fitness and a positive self-perception help us feel closer to our ideal image of ourselves. Some have even noted the most consistent effect of physical exercise on children is their increased self-esteem and improved self-image. There is a long-term effect too as physical activity at ages 9 and 11 predicted self-esteem at ages 11 and 13. With girls as young as five being found to convey dissatisfaction with their body shape and size, it seems essential to focus on self-esteem early.

These developmental and psychological benefits which come from regularly taking part in exercise suggest that children should be highly encouraged to be active, and yet the number of children actually exercising falls way below the recommended guidelines. If we can understand what (and who) influences children to exercise, we should be able to spot those barriers which will need to be moved or mitigated as well as increasing focus on the facilitators and motivators that can help children to exercise.

INDIVIDUAL INFLUENCES ON EXERCISE LEVELS

There are a number of demographic elements which influence how much exercise a child is likely to do. Those who do the least amount of physical activity are those who are overweight or obese and girls. Culture can also have an impact, with some countries or cultures providing physical education only for boys and actively discouraging girls from participating, or placing cultural norms in expecting girls to work harder academically and rewarding boys for sporting achievements.

Self-concept comes into play here as another influence. A child's self-concept will include their perceived ability to perform sports or exercises. This may include the stereotypes which have come from their demographic, so the expectations and norms (being female, being overweight or from a specific culture) give an automatic perception of there being a barrier to exercise. This can also feed into a child's belief and values around exercise which correlate positively with time spent engaging in sports. If children believe in the importance of exercise and value the time spent doing it, they will complete more of it.

An important influence, and one which is often a barrier, is the child's perception of the costs of exercise. This isn't around monetary cost to do activities (though of course that can be an issue in lower socio-economic groups) but the physical (energy, discomfort, effort) and psychological (judgement) costs that can come into play when we exercise. When children have been asked why they hold back from exercising, they have stated that (alongside the environmental barriers such as no friends to go with or lack of motivation) they have a preference for sedentary activities, they lack energy or time and they fear teasing or criticism from others. They are making valid points as being physically active reduces their free time to do the sedentary activities they prefer; teasing will reduce their happiness and sometimes exercise can be uncomfortable. All these elements have a 'cost' associated with them that some children will feel is not worth paying.

ENVIRONMENTAL INFLUENCES ON EXERCISE LEVELS

A significant amount of children's time is spent at school. School has traditionally been a place where exercise was undertaken both in physical education lessons and during break times. Where exercise is taken seriously and valued in schools, it can be a key route to ensuring children stay active enough. However, there are regular warnings that exercise is not valued enough and is the first thing to be cut from the timetable when there are too many competing demands on teachers' time, too much to be covered within the curriculum and additional testing required. Budget cuts also put pressure on the purchasing of play equipment and the cost of insurance and liability protection, resulting in children missing out on the opportunity to do even minimum amounts of exercise in school.

Another key environmental influence on children's levels of activity are their parents. Parents who highly value physical activity are more likely to develop their children's passion towards exercise. Studies have found that the beliefs and values of parents effect not only their children's beliefs and values around exercise but also their actual sports participation to the extent that the children of parents who are both active are 5.8 times more likely to be active than those with inactive parents (Moore et al., 1991). When parents show a passion for sport, their children will put in more effort, take on more difficult tasks and are more likely to intrinsically love the sport for itself rather than what they can get from it. Alongside this, the frequency and type of feedback children receive about their physical activity from those they have significant relationships with (such as parents) also influences their perceived competence and intrinsic motivation to participate in sport.

INCREASING EXERCISE LEVELS IN CHILDREN

Understanding both the barriers and facilitators can help us to design effective exercise programmes and marketing tactics to help children develop a love (or certainly a like) of exercise. Two specific groups to focus upon would be those who are obese and girls as they have the lowest levels of physical exercise at this period of their lives. Being overweight is a marker of chronic inactivity, so overweight, sedentary children will really benefit from exercise, especially as two of the factors contributing to their obesity are low physical activity and/or increasing adaptation to a sedentary lifestyle. With the numbers of children falling into the obese category increasing – already a third of US 6–11 year olds are overweight or obese (Barlow, 2007) – then it becomes imperative that we make physical activity more engaging for them. The other group we need to engage are young girls as they are far less likely to reach recommended activity targets than boys (43% compared to 51% in the UK; Sport England, 2019). For both groups if we are able to capture their interest early, then they may stay more engaged for life.

KEY PROGRAMME ELEMENTS

Self-Determination Theory (see Chapter 1) can offer a strong model to shape interventions in children's exercise as the three pillars (competence, relatedness and autonomy) not only satisfy children's basic needs but also support long-term motivation, which is essential as they are not yet old enough to understand the importance of exercise purely for health and developmental benefits. The more their self-determined needs are met through exercise the more intrinsic their motivation should become, making the children more likely to maintain their newly developed exercise habits.

To start using this approach with children we need to develop their mastery levels. When we are competent in the exercise we choose, we are able to achieve our desired outcome and feel like we have control over the result of our actions. High motor competence in an exercise environment can contribute to engagement, high effort, persistence and enjoyment. As perceived physical competence is lower among overweight or obese children and children with high motor competence spend more time being physically active, boosting the competence levels of overweight children could improve activity levels.

Tactics to help children improve their competence in physical activity skills can include activities tailored to individual capabilities, realistic goal setting, self-management skills and lots of positive and helpful feedback. Offering activities which are tailored to their current capabilities but stretch them a little can also increase their perceived competence and make them feel more inclined to continue. With an activity chosen, helping a child to set a realistic short-term goal will mean they feel successful and start to develop mastery over the basics of their activity. In setting a goal the child can help to plan their own activities, which helps with the feeling of autonomy and their own self-management skills.

Facilitating autonomy is the next element of using a self-determination approach. Children will experience autonomy when they perceive they are in an environment where they can exercise without feeling pressured, their opinions are welcomed and non-controlling language is used. Offering choice can do this and has been found to be more effective than simply providing a specific exercise prescription. If children have choice, they will settle on an activity which they perceive to be fun and pleasurable. When they find a sport or activity they enjoy, have a passion for and have an intrinsic motivation for it, they are more likely to incorporate it long term into their lives. This may be why enjoyment has been associated with higher participation in physical activities in overweight children. Part of enabling choice can be through education, letting children learn and identify their own reasons to be physically active and weigh up their perceptions of the benefits and barriers of physical activity. From this they can set their own goals; so they choose the activity, and if possible when, where and with whom they want to do it; then they can decide what they want to achieve within that activity and by when they feel it would be realistic to do it.

To elicit more consistent levels of exercise in these groups, structured exercise or sports need have a triple focus: to be designed with enjoyment in mind, dedicated to fundamental skill building and set up to highlight personal achievement. This could help to override the feelings of low competence which can come from engaging in a sport that is either unsuited to their body shape or ability or is completely new.

The final element of developing self-determination is relatedness, that perception of belonging and having a meaningful connection to others, feeling understood, cared for, accepted and valued. If children feel part of a community, the programme can be more successful. Clubs can be a good way to do this, but it needs to be a club which suits the level and outlook of the child. Putting a novice swimmer into a competitive team environment will simply highlight that they lack competence and feel left out, thus leaving them very unmotivated. Outside of club systems, school sports teams or activities can be helpful, especially as those from low-income communities often do not have the opportunity to do structured physical activity outside of school. Doing physical education within school gives the additional benefit that it introduces children to new sports or activities and helps them develop the physical literacy that boosts their competency, so they feel more confident in being active outside of school hours.

REDUCING THE PHYSICAL 'COST' OF EXERCISE

Alongside helping children to feel their exercise engagement is self-determined, it is also important to help them handle the difficulties which intense physical activity can bring. An example of this is how some overweight children will be initially limited in their ability to perform some activities such as weight-bearing activities, so offering activities where the children can be active but within a range which doesn't extract too much 'physical cost' until they have built fitness and lost some weight will help them to see that exercise is within their capabilities. Less intense, non-weight-bearing exercise such as cycling, swimming or other aquatic activities can be focused upon in the early stages of a weight reduction program in obese children, however, ideally in their own group so they do not feel judged or worry about comparisons over body size.

A further way to reduce the physical 'cost' may be through distraction. Distraction techniques which reduce the children's perception of effort may tone down their feelings against exercise. Attentional distraction by music might be a useful technique here as the distraction means an increase exercise intensity can be achieved without increasing physical complaints or annoyance as the exercise process becomes more attractive and the music distracts the children from negative bodily sensations.

INTERVENTION IN ACTION: MINI MERMAIDS

A programme ticking many of the best practice boxes around offering competency, facilitating relatedness and reducing the physical cost of exercise is the Mini Mermaids programme. Hannah Corne, the programme CEO, says that until the age of seven, girls and boys see themselves as the same, but at that point they start to become more aware of their perceived differences which are fed to them by society. "Their language changes. They are more exposed to YouTube and social media. Girls start to think that their voices are valued less. Exercise declines at nine and for the majority, it halts completely by 13. The government funded work for keeping girls in exercise starts at about the age of 14 and that is too late. We need to address it early before it gets worse. The girls we work with are helped to see themselves as strong, to be loud, to take up space. They're taught to do things like the power pose. They can see that exercise and sport can be for them."

She uses Azmir as an example of the benefits a programme like Mini Mermaids can bring. Azmir is seven and lives in Leeds. She hates school physical education classes as she and her friends don't like changing in the same room as the boys, and they have to use the school dining hall for PE lessons when there are still bits of food on the floor from lunchtime. They all feel the choice of physical activity is dull and too safe. When a Mini Mermaid programme was set up in her school every Thursday, she wanted to join in but she had to be at mosque at 5 pm, and her father couldn't see how she could take part in Mini Mermaids and be at mosque in time.

The Mini Mermaids team identified this barrier and talked to the school about how to accommodate all the girls who wanted to take part in the programme. The school allowed the girls to finish a bit early on Thursday, so all the girls who wanted to would be able to join the sessions and still make it to mosque.

Over the eight weeks of the programme Azmir and her friends learnt mindfulness, goal setting, got time to celebrate their strengths, see how to help others and find out how to reframe their negative thoughts. They learnt about their bodies and that there is no bad food, that instead what is required, in everything across life, is balance. Everything was focused around physical games and activities so that they learnt that by working hard and sticking with it, they can become fit enough to complete a 5k challenge at their own pace. All of this was done in a fun way where the girls were unaware they were officially learning 'mental skills.' At the end of the programme, Azmir and the other girls completed the 5k by running, walking, hopping and skipping, accompanied by a mentor who was there to listen to them and help them finish. While this was reward enough, the programme also gave them a medal and a personal letter from their coach. The letter reminds them of their strengths, all they have achieved and the barriers they have overcome.

When Azmir completed her 5k, she was watched by both her parents and her siblings. She not only enjoyed being part of the Mini Mermaids' community, but she also helped introduce her family to that community. She got more autonomy by understanding her own body and finding her own voice, and she became more physically competent, all things that should help consolidate habitual exercise into her life and give her confidence in the future. After completing the programme, she said, "now I feel comfortable in my own skin and have learnt how to accept my true self. Mini Mermaids teaches you to be strong and never give up."

3

THE PSYCHOLOGY OF EXERCISE IN TEENAGERS

As children become teenagers, their exercise levels drop. Some suggest this drop starts as early as seven, which means by the time they are teens, at least 81% do not meet the current recommendations for adequate daily physical activity of at least 60 minutes (Guthold, Stevens, Riley, & Bull, 2020). In the US, teenagers doing both moderate and vigorous physical activity declines to only 38 minutes on weekdays and 41 minutes on weekends (Nader, Bradley, Houts, McRitchie, & O'Brien, 2008) with girls dropping down their amounts earlier than boys.

Unhelpfully, at this point when exercise levels are dropping, teenagers enter a key risk period for developing obesity, which doesn't just have an immediate impact but has been found to be pretty stable and continues right into adulthood. During this period our developmental systems rapidly change. The neuroplasticity of our brains means that systems within it are adapting to match new requirements coming from developments in pubertal maturation, social changes (new schools and friends) and neurological advancements. These changes can be stressful, and when under high levels of stress, our bodies become more efficient at storing energy, thus increasing our obesity risk. This risk, alongside prompts from overeating and genetic susceptibility, is also increased by a lack of physical activity. A study of over 5,000 low-income teens in the US found the number of athletic activities they participated in was directly associated with a significant reduction in the likelihood of being overweight or obese and the better they are at regulating their weight (Elkins, Cohen, Koralewicz, & Taylor, 2004).

Obesity is a risk factor for sleep apnoea, type 2 diabetes, cardiovascular disease, stroke, liver and gallbladder disease, depression, social rejection and mortality. Obesity rates in adolescents have increased significantly. In the 40 years between 1965 and 2006, obesity rates for teenagers tripled from 5% to 17.6% (Ogden, Carroll, & Flegal, 2008) and now represents one of the most significant health problems confronting adolescents today. As studies have found that habits, values and lifestyles around exercise formed as a teenager tend to stay with them throughout life, it is important that obesity levels are lowered in adolescence so as not to facilitate long-term risks which increase mortality across their whole lifespan.

THE BENEFITS OF EXERCISING AS A TEEN

Those teenagers who participate in sports spend more of their leisure time exercising or engaging in more vigorous activities, have better physical health-related outcomes with higher cardiovascular fitness, healthy cholesterol and stronger bones. They are also better able to shape their cognitive, communicative, and social skills.

The significant advantages to our mental processes and cognitive behaviours coming from exercising that we saw in childhood have not been identified to the same level within adolescence, but there are still benefits. After cognitively demanding exercise tasks (like circuit training or football skills), students were better able to learn, be creative and concentrate and focus. Those participating in sports also have higher educational aspirations, educational attainment and improved grades. Beyond these specifics that help in education, key life skills such as cooperation, self-discipline, coping in success and adversity, competitiveness, sportsmanship, leadership and self-confidence can be developed through physical activity as a teenager.

Participation in sports during adolescence is associated with better mental health. Teenagers who exercise have lower levels of stress, depression and anxiety. The mental health benefits can be seen right across the board, not just reducing clinical mental health symptoms but positively improving emotional wellbeing, energy levels, mood and happiness. And when there is inactivity, the impact is severe. In a British study of over 4,000 teenagers, it was found that in many teens sedentary behaviour was replacing light activity, and this was putting them at greater risk of depressive symptoms (Kandola, Lewis, Osborn, Stubbs, & Hayes, 2020).

The emotional wellbeing of teenagers can be yet more enhanced when they have higher levels of self-esteem, positive self-perception, increased self-belief, improved body image and self-image. It has been suggested that these improvements come from the psychosocial mechanisms built into sport and exercise, offering opportunities for self-evaluation, peer comparison and healthy competition.

Finally, a long-term benefit of exercising as a teenager is that the habits they build now can last a lifetime. We consistently find that those who participate in sports during childhood have increased physical activity later in life and often better health too. A longitudinal study conducted with Finnish adolescents saw regular sport participation in 14-year olds was linked to higher levels of physical activity 17 years later (Tammelin, Näyhä, Laitinen, Rintamäki, & Järvelin, 2003). A study of Flemish girls aged 12–18 years old found participation in sports during adolescence was a good predictor of involvement in sports nearly 20 years later (Scheerder et al., 2006). It is suggested that this long-term engagement comes because those participating in sports when school aged may develop greater senses of initiative or value their body more than non-athlete counterparts by virtue of their participation and so will continue to engage in healthier behaviours as they age.

INFLUENCES ON TEENAGERS' EXERCISE ENGAGEMENT

Adolescence is a significant phase in the development of our self-perception as our bodies change and our social awareness rises. For some, the desire to improve their self-perception can act as a motivator, but for many it actually behaves as a significant barrier to exercise.

Elements which act as a barrier include high levels of body shame, social physique anxiety and body image dissatisfaction. Body dissatisfaction can affect more than 80% of females and 40% of males (Kostanski & Gullone, 1998), and it can be influenced by tangible, objective factors like a high BMI but also from a perceived social response or comparisons such as teasing or criticisms from others.

Pressures to achieve a socially desirable physique are pervasive and become particularly apparent during this period. For teenage girls the social desirability focuses on thinness. Physical activities which involve tight fitting or revealing outfits, such as swimming and gymnastics, or that objectify the female body like cheerleading can make girls incredibly self-conscious and increase body image dissatisfaction. They may feel objectified or embarrassed, which either reduces their participation or ceases it entirely. Even if the girls are not actually being objectivised, they feel they are and so continually monitor their outward appearance, increasing their appearance anxiety. This isn't just a perceptual issue though; it is socio-cultural, and it is during adolescence when the importance of femininity becomes heightened, and exercise has sometimes been seen as incompatible with that.

Body dissatisfaction may occur less often in males, but when it does, it is often related to ideals around muscularity. It is estimated that up to 47% of boys pursue greater muscularity (Krowchuk, Kreiter, Woods, Sinal, & DuRant, 1998). The pursuit of this may act as a motivator to exercise initially but can have some negative health outcomes along the way, such as poorer body image satisfaction, disordered eating and steroid use. Extreme levels can prompt muscle dysmorphia where teenagers' dedication to building muscle from this socio-cultural pressure to be muscular interferes with their physical health and socio-emotional functioning.

This area of self-perception, body shame and body image dissatisfaction is particularly important as they have they have all been linked at some level to increased risk of eating disorders and the emergence of depressive symptoms and suicidal ideation.

A further area of influence as to the levels of exercise undertaken is around social control and how much autonomy a teenager has. Social control, the deliberate efforts to influence and regulate someone else's behaviours, can act as a barrier to exercise engagement when negative social control strategies are employed, such as ridiculing, pressuring, and making unflattering comparison. Instead of telling a teenager what to do and when to do it, we can provide information, lots of choices and model positive health behaviours. This should increase their motivation to exercise.

Other facilitators which motivate teens to exercise include feeling competent when exercising, believing we can resist more tempting activities (like computer games or sedentary behaviours), living in a safe neighbourhood and actually enjoying exercising. There are also other factors which tend to prompt positive exercise behaviours which do not have a direct link to health or wellbeing, but studies have found they tend to promote health habits. Gender is one such influence, with teenage boys doing significantly more exercise than girls, and a parent's education level is another, positively predicting physical activity levels. Beyond this, coming from a higher socio-economic status, feeling positive and committed towards school, having friends in youth and community groups, engaging in social activities and attending church have all been found to influence teens to do more exercise.

INFLUENCERS ON TEENAGERS' EXERCISE ENGAGEMENT

During adolescence teenagers undergo a developmental transition from a high degree of parental control to an increase in independence and autonomy. They develop an increasing regard for the opinions of others and have heightened neural activation in response to social stimuli, leaving them more susceptible to peer influence, especially as increased freedoms mean that teenagers start to spend increasingly more time with their friends than their families.

A specific change when puberty occurs is that neurobiological developments give an increased sensitivity to oxytocin within the brain which is connected to a variety of social behaviours such as social bonding and heightened attention to positive social stimuli. This may be why, when their peers are supportive towards exercise, other teenagers will be more engaged. On the less positive side this heightened peer attention offers more opportunities to share and compare, which may not always be motivational. In fact, it can be particularly harmful for girls as the more they talk to and engage in appearance comparisons with other girls, the higher their own dissatisfaction grows with their bodies. They also feel that boys hinder their ability to be active, with negative reactions from boys such as teasing and taunting being regularly mentioned as a barrier, especially if they come while playing sport.

Parents do still have a part to play in the adoption of healthy behaviours though, with fathers having been found to have a stronger influence on the physical activity of their teenagers and mothers on their nutrition.

Teachers can also be social change agents, motivating by supporting students with autonomy in their exercise choices, asking the right questions, paying attention to the teenager's opinions and providing choice and opportunities to work independently.

Finally the media that the teenager consumes will also have a strong influence, either as a barrier or facilitator of exercise, so this needs to be taken into account as studies have found the media is a strong contributor of weight-related concerns of young people by relaying weight and appearance-related information via the transmission of the thin beauty ideal.

PRINCIPLES OF TEENAGE EXERCISE INTERVENTIONS

Developing specific programmes to engage teenagers can be effective, and successful ones have prompted healthier lifestyles and lower rates of obesity. There are a number of fundamental principles behind the most successful interventions which could be incorporated into future activities.

EMPOWERMENT

Empowerment-based designs can be employed with teenagers. These interventions focus more on a teenager's strengths and capabilities than on their weaknesses. They can be used to help teens develop a positive body image, become more aware of their own interests and needs, maintain a focus on enjoyment and build self-control, set goals and improve decision-making. The elements of choice contained within these types of programmes provide a strong feeling of control, which is so vital for their motivation and has been found to be an effective way to improve teenagers' self-efficacy towards exercise. Running these types of empowerment programmes in combination with discussions and education on the role and function of the body can help teenagers develop more positive feelings of competence, self-worth and acceptance. The discussions can either take place through group work or motivational interviewing which can strengthen their motivation to change and enhance the likelihood of maintaining positive health behaviours. This process aims to create an atmosphere of acceptance and compassion and focuses attention on the language of change so that the teenager's motivation to their personally set goal is enhanced.

LIMIT COMPARISONS

Twenty percent of teenage girls do their exercise in a gym rather than through sport (Slater & Tiggemann, 2011), but as studies have found that those in the gym have higher levels of body shame and more symptoms of disordered eating, perhaps other environments might be more beneficial. The features of a gym which elevate body dissatisfaction (like lots of mirrors, posters of ideal bodies and the expectation to wear tight and revealing exercise clothing) can be avoided in other environments. Setting interventions in a sport setting or a fitness hall could avoid some of these issues to set up more consistent and health exercise habits and make the sessions feel more inviting.

Ideally, we would start interventions young so that basic competencies and skills can be developed. When teenagers start significantly later than others, comparisons are unavoidable and can feel like a high bar to entry. Where teenagers are starting in sports much later than others of their age, any signposting to clubs needs to ensure they are open for all participants rather than just elite, already well-skilled athletes. Without this in place, novice exercisers may feel very despondent.

When social comparisons can be used in a helpful way, the group being worked with are at an advantage (of which they are unaware). Once they start exercising and realising their advantage, it can give them confidence and boost their motivation. For example, obese teenagers often have high levels of competence within strength training. Highlighting their abilities in this area against those of a healthier weight may improve their self-worth.

UTILISE PEER INFLUENCE

Studies on the brains of teenagers while they make decisions find that it is not until later in adolescence that the systems in their brains mature, allowing them to develop their capacity to coordinate affect and cognition and exercise self-regulation. What can help is the presence of peers as this primes a reward-sensitive motivational state that increases subjective values of immediately available rewards. This increases preferences for short-term benefits, so if we want to get teens exercising, peer influence is a good way to do it. But it is important that this peer influence is pleasant and positive if we want teenagers to stay in programmes.

PARENTAL LEADERSHIP

Peers become far more important as influencers during the teenage years, but parents can still have some influence, so their education and knowledge is important for the effectiveness of interventions. Self-efficacy, proactive behaviours and wellbeing can all be improved through positive parental role modelling and behaviours when parents act as role models, communicate high expectations, show optimism about what can be achieved, encourage their teens to contribute their own thoughts and ideas and adapt activities to their teens' specific needs and abilities. To offer transformational leadership parents need high-quality information and knowledge about health and exercise to know what is suitable exercise, and they need to understand how to communicate their thoughts effectively so their teens neither misinterpret their intentions nor believe they are trying to control them.

TECHNOLOGY

Research is starting to emerge around the use of technology and apps in exercise psychology. Teenagers would be a key area for this research and, if positive, to apply interventions using them. However, to date the findings are not particularly positive. While some studies have shown that web-based tailored interventions may be a promising method to promote health behaviours of adolescents, others suggest they may not have yet hit the right note. A study investigating the effects of a mobile physical activity intervention on life satisfaction and self-rated health among young adolescent men found that even though their app helped them set personal objectives for physical activity and fitness improvement, gave instructions and guidelines, and provided tailored, automated health information and messages, the impact was low and 41% did not even use the service (Pyky et al., 2017). An area which is looking more positive, however, is around exercising in a virtual environment, and it will be interesting to see how these types of interventions for teenagers develop.

INTERVENTION IN ACTION: SKATES DAGENHAM

When Diana Thesee was a teenager, she loved skating. She spent hours at the local rink as it was affordable and she loved the freedom it gave her. As an adult, with children of her own and chatting to the teenagers her husband was supporting as a youth worker, she realised the teenage girls around her needed something similar.

"We started talking about it and the girls were really keen but they could see all the barriers; where would they skate, where would they get skates from? We are in a low-income area so the mums wanted their girls to join in but knew they couldn't afford a high entry fee or to buy the skates. It was important to me it was accessible and affordable to the girls so I approached a charity called Community Resources and we applied for funding. The funding we got covers the purchase of the skates, the wrist guards and hall hire. All the girls pay is £1 a session."

The Skating Club has now been running for two years. "There are a core of 10–15 girls who attend every week and then they may bring friends along too. We've grown through word of mouth."

There are a wide range of benefits which don't just help the girls' fitness and wellbeing but make the skating something they really commit to. Thesee has loved watching friendships develop among the girls. "When they first came there were three different groups and they didn't talk to each other. Now they have all developed a shared bond. They have a snapchat group and meet up outside of Skates too." It is the ability to develop these friendships which has helped their mental health. "The girls say it is a stress reliever to come and skate and have a chat too and get things off their chest. So, the fitness is great but it is also about their mental wellbeing. It is so good emotionally and we play games on the skates so the girls really get to know each other."

The girls feel safe at Skates. "The building is a safe building. Once in, the doors are shut and each week it is me and the same volunteers so they can trust us. Being an all girls session means they feel they can be totally themselves and because the same girls coming every week so they know everyone and feel comfortable here."

Their confidence has been boosted too. Some of this is down to the abilities they have developed on wheels. "Most of the girls have bought their own skates now so some have started roller skating outside and others are so good they are moving onto jumps. It is amazing to see their progress." Developing this competence in their activities means low self-esteem has been boosted. "One mum said her daughter had never been able to commit to anything before and yet she now comes every week.

"For many of the girls there is nothing else for them to do and they don't take part in any other physical activity. Having something active and safe to do should be available for everyone. We get to see how much they enjoy coming and how much they appreciate it. We have occasionally invited along girls where they have self-harmed or had depression or anxiety and they thrive – you can see a real growth in how they feel about themselves because it makes them part of something. It gives them a sense of achievement and better wellbeing. It means they belong and this is really important."

4

THE PSYCHOLOGY OF EXERCISE IN ADULTS

To benefit from the physical and psychological effects of exercise it is recommended that adults do at least five 30-minute bouts of moderate to vigorous physical activity each week. A relatively small number of us actually achieve this, as low as 29% in some parts of the world (Hallal et al., 2012). The economic and health burdens related to these low levels of exercise have become a global public health concern, with physical inactivity being one of the leading risk factors for global mortality with approximately 3.2 million deaths (6%) per year being attributed to it.

Regular physical activity is protective against several chronic diseases, such as cardiovascular disease, diabetes, cancer, hypertension, stroke, obesity, depression and osteoporosis, and against premature death. A set of 14 studies (covering over 230,000 participants) found that those who run regularly have a 27% lower risk of all-cause mortality, a 30% lower risk of cardiovascular disease and a 23% lower risk of cancer (Pedisic et al., 2019). They found even running just once a week could be beneficial. But exercise doesn't just protect against poor health; it also improves general health, both physical and mental.

Exercise has been found to be extremely beneficial for our brain's cognitive performance, facilitating changes in our brain activity and brain function. It is thought that when we exercise, we increase our capillary blood supply to the cortex from which new neurons and synapses grow, resulting in better learning and performance. Studies have found that, right across the adult age group, moderate-intensity aerobic exercise (around 30 minutes of it) will facilitate better cognitive performance. Even acute, short-term bouts of resistance or moderate-intensity exercise can improve cognitive performance, including planning and problem-solving, and beyond cognitive function, improved mood and higher levels of self-esteem have been noted.

If someone has a mental health issue, then exercise can be helpful at reducing the symptoms and impact. Depression is one of the leading causes of years lived with disability, and anti-depressants are only effective for about 60% of the population (Rush et al., 2006). Exercise can improve the psychological quality of life in people with depression, to the equivalent level of using anti-depressants. It has also been found to be valuable at reducing stress and anxiety levels.

The social benefits are strong too. Being more active and engaged with others has a huge positive impact on our quality of life, which links to our life satisfaction and length of life. Really positively the benefits can be experienced by people even if they have only just started exercising after a long period of inactivity, so it is never too late to start.

While these benefits are enticing, the barriers that we face and our ability to adapt or cope with them are actually a better prediction of whether we are likely to exercise, as we know that those who perceive a high number of barriers and consider there are only a few benefits are those who do the least exercise.

BARRIERS TO EXERCISE

Many adults have a huge number of 'pulls' upon their time. Unless they have built exercise into a habit, genuinely enjoy it and have internalised the benefits, these pulls can make exercise really tricky to adhere to. The barriers they individually face will reflect their socio-economic status, their previous experience, long-term attitudes to exercise, current lifestyle and family situation, environment, priorities, responsibilities and physical and mental status. We can address each of these in terms of different types of cost: financial, fatigue, lifestyle, psychological and incentive.

While some types of exercise are very cheap (such as running or walking), there can still be significant financial barriers, especially to finding a form of exercise you love. Costs of exercise are not just membership fees for gyms or sports clubs but competition or match fees, equipment needed and indirect costs such as travel and sportswear. Financial costs have been specifically identified as a barrier in older adults, those with low income and those with weight concerns, with over 75% of respondents in a study of those with a high BMI and a low economic status saying they needed activities at little or no cost (Burton, Khan, & Brown, 2012).

The physical cost of exercise either from tiredness or health issues is another barrier to consider. Where someone feels fatigued due to their work and lifestyle and believes they do not have enough additional energy to exert themselves physically, it can become a vicious circle. Their poor health becomes a barrier to regular exercise, and then not being a regular exerciser creates even more poor health.

Our lifestyle changes as we move through different periods in our lives. For adults the two key lifestyle changes will come as they enter adulthood (when they go through a number of demographic changes, such as leaving home and becoming financially independent) and if they become parents. Becoming a parent impacts men's exercise levels a little but women's exercise levels significantly more as they struggle to find the time and energy to exercise once children are on the scene. First-time mothers show a significantly larger decrease in exercise in the first year of their child's life, and they commonly report that family priorities, care-giving duties, and lack of time and physical fatigue were barriers to participation in exercise. The more children a woman has the less exercise she feels able to do. If, however, new mums believe that exercise increases energy, relieves stress and makes them feel better, they will exercise more. This suggests that education on the benefits of exercise in actually reducing tiredness and feelings of fatigue could be valuable for new mums.

A further lifestyle barrier is where you live. Those in disadvantaged areas are much more likely (and probably for good reason) to perceive their neighbourhood as unattractive and unsafe, which can restrict the type of activities they feel able to try. When nearby venues are unsuitable and the financial or time cost of travel to other facilities is not feasible, it becomes a large barrier. Unsurprisingly those who live in places where there are lots of walkability and street connectivity, great transport, good aesthetics and lots of recreation facilities tend to do more exercise.

The psychological cost of exercise can also create a barrier, particularly to those whose self-identity doesn't match that of an exerciser. It may be that they don't feel competent in the exercise they are attempting, which reduces their likelihood of attempting it as we favour doing activities we are good at. It may also be the case that, for those who don't feel comfortable with their current body shape or size, physical activity can feel embarrassing and intimidating, and this has been found to reduce frequency of visits to the gym.

Finally, there can be a low incentive cost when our previous exercise experiences were associated with displeasure and we still don't find exercise enjoyable. Even worse, when we find it boring, it can become a major barrier to participation as not only do many of the other costs come into play, but we know we won't even like doing it once we've overcome those barriers.

FACILITATORS OF EXERCISE

To increase the success of any exercise programme it is important to be able to tap into what motivates people, so understanding the facilitators of exercise for adults can be really beneficial.

Genetics plays a part. Numerous studies have demonstrated the heritability of exercise behaviour, with a twin – sibling study looking at over 5,000 twins and siblings aged between 18 and 50 (Huppertz et al., 2014). A significant genetic contribution was found for exercise behaviour (50% in males, 43% in females) and for barriers to exercise take-up, such as lack of skills, support and/or resources, time constraints, lack of energy, lack of enjoyment and embarrassment. One of the elements of this heritably may be the part that personality plays. Personality traits are partly genetic, and extraversion and conscientiousness have been specifically linked to positive exercise behaviours.

We might imagine that setting the right goals for exercise impacts how much of it we do, and there is some truth in this, but an element which has a bigger predictive impact is 'why.' Why does someone intend to do the exercise? This is especially strong when their 'why' matches their personal values. This 'why' is our motivation. As younger people much of our motivation for exercise is extrinsically based; we are exercising because we are told to in physical education classes, or there is a match to win for our school. Once we are in our 20s and are beyond the direct influence of others, whether or not we choose to exercise will be highly influenced by how intrinsically motivated we are to do it.

The research shows that when we begin our journey (the preparation and action stages) into exercise as adults (if we haven't continued doing it from childhood), we are often quite extrinsically motivated; we are doing it to look better or be fitter or to meet new people. Once we move into the maintenance stage, our motives internalise and our motivation becomes more autonomous. To get to the maintenance stage though, we need to become adept in regulating our behaviours (elements we use daily such as action planning or determination) and hone our abilities to commit to a goal and stick with it. The positive interaction of our exercise motives and psychological wellbeing helps to reinforce our positive feelings, and so exercise feels more intrinsically rewarding. This is important as extrinsic motives for exercise are thought to lead to stress in individuals, whereas intrinsic motives are thought to lead to a release of stress.

Our own body shape and size is also seen as having a key influence on our exercise behaviours. The dissatisfaction many of us have with how we perceive our body (our body image) is now so prevalent that it is considered a normative discontent, and anyone deviating from the youthful body ideal may struggle. Older adults as they put on weight, reduce muscle, lose hair and may begin to use hearing, seeing, and mobility aids will be impacted. Anyone who is overweight may struggle too, as almost 75% of those with a high BMI indicate a preference for activities that can be done alone, saying it was difficult to enjoy structured physical activity if they were not an 'ideal shape and size' (Burton et al., 2012). Media and social interactions can continually remind us how our bodies deviate from the young ideal, posing a constant threat to our body image and, depending on our motivation and personality, can push us to exercise in order to control it or, like those in the high BMI study, avoid exercise to ignore it.

Being physically active as a child also has a huge impact on whether we remain physically active as we enter adulthood. A Finnish study that tracked participants for 21 years found that persistent participation in youth sport means someone is five times more likely to still be physically active at the age of 30 (Telama, Yang, Hirvensalo, & Raitakari, 2006). The younger we start the more likely we are to still be exercising in adulthood. One reason for this might be that we maintain our competency in our activity so feel more comfortable to continue. Another is that the positive self-beliefs of long-term exercisers means they develop a self-identity as someone who is active and fit. Adults don't just need to have been active as a youth to get the high self-esteem and continued engagement, they also needed to see the sporting experience as high quality and full of enjoyable memories. So it is not just the amount of exercise we have done in the past or what type but how much we enjoyed it and how supportive and encouraging our coaches were.

Gender also plays an important part in our exercise behaviours. Men do more exercise on average than women, and evolutionary perspective studies suggest this might be a result of sex-specific workout behaviours based on competition for mates. Their suggestion is that men try to look larger and women try to look smaller as we tend to view largeness as more masculine and smallness as more feminine. Whether evolutionary or as a result of social learning, this drive to adopt a culture of thinness and musculature can be seen to influence motivations – men most by intrinsic factors (strength, competition and challenge) and women by extrinsic factors (weight management and appearance).

A final area of influence comes from the social support we have. Researchers have found for some groups, such as those who are socio-economically disadvantaged, that exercising with others is actually much more important to them than the exercise as it facilitates the social support networks which they might otherwise miss.

PRINCIPLES OF ADULT EXERCISE INTERVENTIONS

In order to prevent, reduce, treat and control the negative health outcomes of physical inactivity, programmed exercise interventions have shown to be useful. The big challenge is to develop physical activity programmes that can be implemented in a cost-effective and sustainable way which is also engaging and supporting, so people develop adherence to prevent the high levels of dropout which often come in the first few months of a programme.

Participation can be increased by offering choice of what type and how intensely people get to exercise, having activities and facilities close to home, including ways to increase physical self-esteem, offering both unstructured activities and those which can be done alone. There are also a number of other key principles which, if incorporated into interventions, may well improve the likelihood of adults taking up and maintaining an exercise habit.

UNDERSTANDING MOTIVATION

A key element required for success within exercise initiation and adherence is finding our why, nailing down our motivation. If we understand our motive for exercise, we can tailor programmes better to our needs and find activities that suit our personal profile for participation. Different types of motivation have an impact. Extrinsic motivations (based on others or external reasons such as social recognition, affiliation or competition) will result in poorer psychological wellbeing. Intrinsic motivations (based on our enjoyment, love of the exercise or friends we see when doing it) will lead to better psychological wellbeing and longer-term engagement.

The motivation we have to take up exercise may well differ to what keeps us maintaining that habit. We tend to start off exercising for extrinsic motives, but we maintain exercise when we develop intrinsic motivation and become more competent, develop feelings of enjoyment and see the benefits it has to our wellbeing. These feelings help us develop behavioural reinforcement, controlled via the central dopamine system which allows us to increase how much we do.

SETTING AND FACILITATING GOALS

Once we understand our motivation, we can set goals. Goals are the cognitive links between our motivation and our specific behaviours. People tend to set approach goals (such as I will exercise to improve my fitness) or avoidance goals (I will exercise so I don't get ill). Approach goals have been found to be more effective as they help us to see progress towards our desirable state. It is important we don't try to set these goals for anyone else though, as the interventions which support the participant designing their own goal, implementation strategy and action plan gives them more autonomy and so is more effective.

We can help facilitate achievement of these goals by using brief imagery exercises which influence behaviours. There are two types that can be used: outcome simulation (generating images of the outcome) and process simulation (generating images of the steps leading to the outcome). If we start with outcome simulation to get the adult to identify specific and concrete goals, we can then move on to using process simulation to set the scene for how that goal will be attained. If the imagery is vivid, uses experiential language to make it come alive and is practiced regularly, it can have a positive impact on changes in physical habits.

OFFER CHOICE

There are hundreds of sports and exercise options for a reason: our physicalities and personalities suit different types of activities. Studies suggest that key elements which shape our choices include: previous experiences (so where we feel competent), whether we are looking for social elements (so gravitate to team sports such as lacrosse, netball, basketball, football or volleyball), if we enjoy higher levels of challenge and competition (taking up racquet sports like tennis, table tennis or squash), whether we are focused on physical condition (aerobics or weight training), if we enjoy body and mind-related skills (martial arts) or whether we have high levels of competence motivation (individual sports such as tennis or running). How we each respond to different types of exercise will translate into our subjective and affective experience influencing levels of take-up and adherence.

To elicit positive affective responses, we need to do exercise which matches at least some of our preferences and is limited as to how much physical discomfort or fatigue it causes. But it shouldn't feel too easy. We need to feel like we are working hard when we exercise to develop confidence in our abilities, something which will help us work harder in the future. Where someone exercises matters too. While many people are put off by outdoor exercise, studies have found we actually tend to exercise for longer when outside than we exercise at home, work or in a gym.

CONSIDER PERSONAL CIRCUMSTANCES

Low-income groups, not surprisingly, prefer low-cost activities. They also prefer non-vigorous, non-competitive indoor activities that are not just about exercise but also involve socialising. Strategies such as loyalty programmes, group discounts, bulk purchasing, financial incentives to promote and reward ongoing participation, and special offers for those on a low income have all been suggested.

Those who are overweight generally prefer activities that are supervised, non-competitive, with people of the same age and gender (to offer a sense of solidarity) and are team based and take place at a fixed time with scheduled sessions. They also indicate a preference for activities which offer high levels of external support and structure and are not just about exercise. The external support can come through encouragement, feedback and education on the importance of participation over mastery or outcome. It can also be provided with individualised instructions on the most suitable type and level of activities while helping individuals set goals and problem-solve their barriers. When this is all set inside for a programme that involves scheduled sessions to create a routine and social commitment, the likelihood of continued physical activity engagement increases.

Studies with those aged over 40 have found they are far keener to exercise alone with very few preferring team sports and many not being interested in competition. When they do exercise with others, they are usually keen to be with others of a similar age.

When working with different genders, men's programmes have found focusing on developing mastery (by learning new skills) and being able to compete in some way (at a level where they experience success) will be beneficial. Women's programmes have found that opportunities which enhance psychological wellbeing and maintaining or enhancing their appearance work best for initiating exercise.

Programmes for those with body image dissatisfaction have found that instead of suggesting coping strategies that work on appearance fixing (such as trying to camouflage or fix an attribute) or avoidance (such as withdrawing from others), there are much better results when using positive rational acceptance, such as more self-care. The individuals using this positive rational acceptance as a coping strategy have lower body image dysfunction, lower likelihood of defining themselves by their physical appearance, more positive body image quality of life, greater self-esteem, slightly lower levels of eating disturbance and greater perceived social support from family and friends, so teaching individuals to appreciate what their body can do and how to care for it well should be a key element of any intervention.

Finally, the parents or carers of young children may need additional support to start and maintain exercise habits due to the many different barriers, roles and calls upon their time.

INTERVENTION IN ACTION: FOOTBALL FANS IN TRAINING (FFIT)

The Football Fans in Training (FFIT) programmes, and programmes that draw heavily on it are now delivered all over the world. It began in Scotland in June 2011 with the aim of helping obese adult men live healthier lives. With many programmes (such as slimming world or weight watchers) aimed at women, FFIT was designed to support men to lose weight by eating better and being more physically active. FFIT is a 12-week, group-based programme delivered by trained coaches. It aimed to support men to achieve at least 45 minutes of moderate-intensity physical activity on most days of the week and to pay attention to the energy balance, with energy in through eating and energy out through physical activity. The programme included a walking programme which allowed men to build up fitness safely and slowly and group-based physical activity sessions. Traditional intervention techniques taught to the men on the programme included self-monitoring through pedometer step counts and setting SMART (specific, measurable, achievable, realistic, time-limited) goals to make sustainable changes.

An analysis of over 700 men who took part in a FFIT programme showed it was effective from both a health and cost perspective. Those on the FFIT programme lost more than nine times as much weight as men who had not done the programme, and a year later 40% of the men on the programme had maintained a weight loss of at least 5% of their original body weight. Participants increased their physical activity levels and improved their diets and psychological wellbeing.

Professor Sally Wyke was one of the lead instigators of the FFIT programme. "The focus was on weight management but we did that through healthy eating and physical activity. It was focused on sustainable behaviour change. Teaching the men a toolbox of behaviour change techniques that they could come back to.

"We partnered with the Scottish Professional Football League Trust to develop a programme that might attract men between 35 and 65. We found some push and pull factors; the main push factor was that men were not happy with their body but didn't know what to do about it. The pull factor was the idea of being invited to the programme in a professional football club with other people like them. The initial hook was the football club but once they were hooked they began to enjoy the sessions, they enjoyed learning from one another, the banter and the physical activity."

FFIT supported the use of different techniques at different times. "At the initiation stage we developed a walking programme and this used self-monitoring. This was an important behaviour change technique as it helped them build up gradually from a baseline and slowly increase their fitness. They were self-monitoring their physical activity and their weight." The second element of their tool kit at this stage was goal setting to both improve eating and physical activity. "The third behaviour change technique was information, which the men enjoyed. For the maintenance stage the programme used planning techniques and 'If . . . Then' Plans."

Everything within FFIT was embedded in a supportive motivational environment. "There is no telling anybody what to do. It just uses what people already know to develop mutual learning. The men fed back that the content was 'science but not rocket science' as they felt they gained control through the information. Being able to work in this experiential way means they feel the benefits as they go along and this helps them stick to the programme."

The programme can be neatly articulated through the pillars of self-determination theory. "There is autonomy by offering choice, facilitating mutual learning and people setting their own goals. There is competence by using group-based reviews where people share how they got on and how they did it and that information is used to change their own practice. The relatedness is supported through interaction; the banter and the sharing of experiences."

Understanding the culture in the area is important. Wyke explained that the programmed worked with, rather than against, men's masculinities. "We would find men would be getting teased about weight loss if they turned down a pint or a bacon sandwich but being able to explain they are doing a programme in the football club gave them a defence against this criticism from their peers."

By considering the content (teaching a toolbox of skills which can be used), style (adult learning techniques involving vicarious learning from each other and their experiences) and delivery (in a supportive environment) the programme could be tailored to the specific audience and see them through the hook, initiation and maintenance. "This means the programme isn't a diet. Instead it becomes a way of life."

5

THE PSYCHOLOGY OF EXERCISE IN RETIREES

As we age and move into our later years, we begin to evaluate our lives, develop greater awareness over the deterioration of our physical health and fear that we will soon need to depend upon others. Those in this stage of life can use exercise to extend their years of active independence, reduce disability and improve their quality of life. High levels of physical functioning are so fundamentally important to healthy aging that participation in exercise and physical activity is a strong predictor of aging well and a protector from some of the stress of the life events that we experience as we age.

The cognitive benefits found in exercise at younger ages still apply for those who are retired. Exercise at this age will still lead to improvements in executive function and cognitive performance, and there are also a growing number of studies looking at the impact of exercise on neurodegenerative health conditions. Studies are finding that physically active older people have a reduced risk of developing Alzheimer's or other forms of dementia. It seems that exercise could be a powerful protective strategy against many of the health declines we tend to expect as we age.

Those joining programmes to improve their health find improvements in cardiovascular fitness, muscular fitness, psychological health, functional capacity and in their quality-of-life indicators. They reduce their levels of loneliness and isolation, have fewer depressive symptoms and find that the habit of regular attendance to a physical activity provides a sense of structure and purpose to their day-to-day lives, something particularly valuable for those recently retired from paid work. Even older people with major depressive disorder have been found to be able to reduce their depressive symptoms with aerobic and strength training.

Despite the numerous benefits, studies have found that as we go through the process of retirement, even though theoretically we have more time to exercise, we actually reduce the amount of physical activity we do. The theory of activity substitution suggests that as people retire, they should have more time to exercise as they gain leisure time. However, it seems there is still significant competition for time, especially around caring responsibilities. The more care that must be provided, the less physical activity is conducted and, as much of this care has fallen to women, it may be a factor in why exercise levels are lower in older women than older men.

The reduced physical activity levels are thought to come from less travel (mainly to and from work) and a lack of routine. Instead of compensating by increasing their leisure-time physical activity, it seems retirees are increasing the amount of time they are sedentary to, on average, 9.4 hours a day (Harvey, Chastin, & Skelton, 2015). It is estimated that the percentage of older adults meeting the recommendations on physical activity is around 22% (Grimm, Swartz, Hart, Miller, & Strath, 2012). Even physical activities such as walking decline significantly when people get to much older ages, and again, the decline is largest in women. This is thought to be a response to musculoskeletal problems and concerns about personal safety.

Positively though, studies have found that those who are about to or who have recently retired are receptive to changing their behaviours, feeling that retirement offers opportunities, specifically additional time, to develop a healthy lifestyle. If we are to use this opportunity as a platform for developing new exercise habits, we need to understand any barriers in place. This is not a simple process as the requirements, wants and influences of this group are complex, especially as in some countries such as the UK there is no longer a 'retirement age,' and so adults retire at different ages, with very different exercise histories. Understanding the psychology of exercise in those who are retiring and have been retired for some time will help those working in this area to support their physical activity needs effectively.

BARRIERS TO EXERCISE IN RETIREES

Barriers, the significant potential obstructions to the adoption, maintenance or resumption of participation in exercise, can be extensive in retirement. Some barriers are fairly physical and need infrastructure support. Others are more perception led, health based, have a social focus or simply come from a place of inertia. Education, marketing and ease of access can help reduce these barriers. The final barrier is time. Despite retirees theoretically having more time to exercise, it is caring responsibilities, volunteer work and an enhanced social calendar that seem to prevent regular activity from being undertaken.

Barriers from the logistical side are around the environment, and they can be extensive. Poor weather, darkness, uneven pavements, intimidating roads, buildings and parks, cars parked on pavements, air pollution, traffic, hills, fear of physical attack in a neighbourhood, fear of crime and a lack of suitable or affordable facilities for sessions nearby can all act as barriers to exercise. Most can be overcome, but it often takes significant effort on the part of the retiree to do so.

Perception issues can sometimes be approached through education. There are beliefs that exercise is too risky at an older age, that there will be discomfort or unpleasant sensations when exercising or that they are receiving conflicting health advice so are unsure of what to do, in which case less is easier and feels safer. There can also be perception issues caused by negative affect where feelings of depression, lack of motivation, reduced willpower or low discipline come into play. Here sometimes there will be links to low self-efficacy, particularly if not having exercised before. Feeling self-conscious, shy, embarrassed, intimidated or worried they won't keep up or not having the right clothes or equipment can all prompt negative self-perception and an invisible but very real feeling barrier, particularly for women.

A significant number of retirees also have health issues which can make physical activity harder. Some of these may be caused by wear and tear, others by lack of fitness and some by chronic or acute illnesses which are more common as one ages. Some retirees who are actually highly motivated to exercise are stopped by injuries as they can occur more often at this age and can take longer to heal. This leaves them not only unable to exercise but also highly frustrated. As well as actual health issues, there can be the threat of health issues that may be prompted by exercise, such as fear of pain or shortness of breath, risk of injury or the fear of falling.

FACILITATORS OF EXERCISE

Studies have found that there seem to be four main areas which influence retirees levels of exercise: personal factors (age, gender, education level, socio-economic class and time free), social and cultural factors (influence of a medical expert, social support and attitude of friends and family, social networks and expectations), environmental factors (type, location, and quality of physical activities; travel time; physical environment, home location and cost) and health (both real and perceived).

Gender can influence the amount of exercise undertaken by older people. There seem to be very different influences of exercise at this age based on gender. A study of 1,303 Finnish individuals aged 57–78 years found 39% of men and 48% of women were doing no moderate or vigorous leisure-time physical activity (Hakola, Hassinen, Komulainen et al., 2015). They found specific factors influencing exercise levels in men were age, marital status, still working, having a weak social network and poor diet. In women, cardiovascular disease and depressive symptoms were the key factors. Two large studies of female retirees in Australia found health and social contact were key to their exercise involvement.

Once adults are past retirement, the more they age, the more likely they are to drop exercise, except if they think of themselves as younger. This influence is based on perception around age and isn't just about how old one perceives themself but their own attitude towards aging. A study of adults between the ages of 50 and 70 found that those who had positive aging expectations were more likely to engage in exercise and consume a healthier diet compared with those who had conventional aging expectations (Huy, Schneider, & Thiel, 2010). Those who assume that health problems are an inevitable consequence of growing old will feel preventive health behaviours (such as exercise) are futile and so do less. And really interestingly there can also be a feeling among a number of retirees that they feel high levels of sedentary behaviour are legitimate at their age, having 'earned' the opportunity to rest after decades of often intense and demanding employment.

Other personal factors which have been found to reduce the levels of exercise in retirement include lower levels of education and lower socio-economic status. Personality can also play a part, with those high in conscientiousness being more active.

Health issues are raised time and time again by participants in studies as influencing how much they exercise. Many of the issues involved are incredibly complex. For some they may act as a motivator and for others a barrier. One element where some generalisations can be made is that those who have poor general health (higher body weight, lower VO2 max, spending lot of time sitting, high depression scores and perceive their health is poor) are those doing the least physical activity. If an older adult believes they have the physical health in place to be active, this will positively influence the levels of activity they do, so self-efficacy can be considered to be a really strong indicator of exercise in this group.

The social environment and social support given, such as friends and family, have consistently been found to influence participation in physical activity in older age, but unfortunately older people generally receive less encouragement from others regarding their exercise habits, possibly because friends and family are nervous about risks.

A way to study where helpful social influence is coming from is to look at social networks. A social network is the collection of meaningful personal ties that individuals maintain, such as relations with family members, friends, neighbours and significant others. Supportive social networks have a positive impact on the maintenance of an exercise programme and on a physically active lifestyle. A study based on the data within the Baltimore Longitudinal Study on Aging (a survey of 6,780 respondents) found that physical activity is associated with having more social-support networks outside of the family (Wolinsky, Stump, & Clark, 1995), and it is those with really diverse social networks who have the highest levels of physical activity.

A wider cultural issue is that retirees can feel excluded and like a 'forgotten group' where nothing is tailored for them. They feel too old for regular exercise programmes and too young for ones focused on older people.

Finally, the environment around retires can either act as a strong enabler of physical activity or a significant block to it. Several studies have found that one of the highest enablers of exercise was having walkable access to amenities; this is important because walking is the main exercise for many older adults. Convenience is also important, with activities being offered closer to home leading to more active lives. Higher levels of physical activity in the community are undertaken when the pavements and gardens are well maintained, when there is less litter, when there is seating, green spaces and accessible locations to exercise. Levels of exercise go down when there are window security bars on residences and high neighbourhood violent-crime rates. This has been found to link to why those in lower socio-economic groups do less exercise; they feel unsafe doing physical activity in their neighbourhoods and have less access to facilities either due to availability or cost.

THE MOTIVATIONS OF RETIREES TO EXERCISE

Understanding exactly what motivates people to become physically active is a key factor in designing effective exercise interventions, and there are some specific studies that can help us understand the strengths of some of these motivators on retirees.

A systematic review of nearly 2,000 participants identified 92 motivators to older people participating in resistance training (Burton et al., 2017). The most frequently identified reasons for commencing and continuing resistance training were health related, but there were also key motivators around longevity and being able to live independently. A French study looking at 92 physically active retirees aged between 63 and 89 backed up this health element, splitting their responders into two groups: those who see physical activity as a high priority to stay healthier longer, to take care of their body and mind and to maintain physical autonomy; and those who come from a risk perspective, using physical activity to prevent falls and fractures and delay the onset of physical frailty (Ferrand, Nasarre, Hautier, & Bonnefoy, 2012).

Interestingly, for studying retirement, age plays a part in motivation to participate in exercise. The middle-age group (55–64) in a study by Kolt, Driver, and Giles (2004) differed significantly in their reasons for participating in exercise to those older than them. They rated social, fitness and challenge reasons significantly higher than participants in any other age group. The 'old-old' group (those over 75) rated medical reasons higher than anyone else.

Even when highly driven to turn motivation into activity, it needs to be easy for people to exercise. Having access to good-quality, cost-effective exercise facilities, activities and equipment, in a convenient location, close to home, staffed by competent professionals with retiree-relevant expertise who are friendly, interactive and encouraging is necessary. Within this it is key there is some element of choice, such as being able to exercise at their own pace, in sports or classes which they enjoy, at a level which is neither too easy nor too advanced for their personal situation and doesn't feel intimidating.

A social side is also important for many. A French study found that when exercising with others, the participants saw it as not only a group activity but also a place where they can meet and communicate with others sharing their experiences (Ferrand et al., 2012). Some used this group for support, others for motivation. If there is a sense of belonging, a feeling they fit in a way to grow friendships while exercising, a sense of vicarious confidence by seeing others like them being active and having a good and non-threatening gym or exercise atmosphere, then retirees feel accepted and engaged. They will want to continue to stay physically active. This social side can then become the glue that binds together the exercise and the exerciser.

PROCESSES TO GET RETIREES EXERCISING

Th moment of retirement could be an ideal stage for implementation of interventions which prevent older adults from lapsing into an inactive lifestyle and from becoming socially excluded. However, with the depth and range of barriers that exist, proactive engagement is required to help older adults find their motivation so they can alter their behaviours to become more active.

A key area for increasing engagement with retirees around the importance of including physical activity in their lives can come through education, specifically the dissemination of accurate information to counter misperceptions such as fear of falling or believing the guidelines for physical activity (150 minutes a week) are too physically demanding and beyond their capabilities. It has been suggested that meetings or booklets are given to adults on retirement to explain the guidelines, the benefits in following them and what motivates others to exercise in case this inspires and offers help in identifying opportunities to achieve more physical activity themselves.

Simply disseminating information about the health benefits of moderate physical activity is not sufficient to increase participation. Instead, working on boosting a retiree's self-efficacy has been found to increase increased exercise participation. It has a circular effect, too, with those who exercise more frequently and who have social support throughout an exercise programme increasing their levels of self-efficacy.

Another element to get retirees exercising can be around highlighting ease of access into physical activity. A large number of studies from a wide range of countries have focused on walking as the most common form of exercise, and others have shown that even a small increase in walking can have significant health benefits. Perhaps a focus on using this method to reach the advised 150 minutes a week will help to get retirees building better exercise habits, and once this is in place, they will have increased their self-efficacy and can add more vigorous exercise into their schedule.

INCREASING ADHERENCE ONCE EXERCISING

Group-based physical activity has been found to be an excellent way to start a physical activity programme, but long-term adherence rates are actually greater in those who engage in individual exercise. In a US study of 3,305 adults, it was clear that older adults and retirees had a strong preference (69%) to exercise alone with some instruction rather than being in a formal group with an exercise leader (Wilcox, King, Brassignton, & Ahn, 1999). Perhaps this is because although older adults prefer a group setting, their activities will be less personalised with this approach, and being able to tailor exercise programs to the needs and interests of participants allows them to initiate and maintain a routine of regular physical activity.

Social support has been found to be both a barrier (when some push for their older family members to take life easier or have caring responsibilities) and a motivation (through exercise buddies, active family and friends or health-education support). Using social support effectively could make adhering to exercise much easier for retirees. One way to achieve this can be through peer mentoring. It is based on the idea that individuals who share common problems have a unique resource to offer one another and that with training and supervision, they can help others. Among older adults, peer mentors have been reported to be empathic and respectful towards one another and through positive role modelling have been found to be able to not only dispel some of the negative stereotypes of aging but also empower participants. When one study investigated the effectiveness of a peer-mentored exercise program on 60 older adults (mean age

69), they found those who were peer mentored improved their fitness significantly and by just as much as those mentored by younger fitness experts.

Something else being trialled is health contracts. A health contract usually includes realistic goal setting and a measurable plan or course of action agreed between the retiree and health professional for reaching health goals. Tools like calendars can be used to record physical activity and help the retiree monitor how well they are doing and reinforce their commitment. Alongside this can be positive reinforcement through social recognition for improvement or success and regular performance feedback. Providing regular and accurate performance feedback can help older adults develop realistic expectations of their own progress. It helps them develop self-efficacy and feelings of competency, both elements which will help them maintain their exercise routine. Feedback needs to be positive, meaningful and offer further direction for the retiree to continue to improve.

Finally, knowing the risk factors for dropout can be valuable as pre-emptive action. A number of risk factors can be identified as to who may drop out of exercise programmes. Dropout levels are often high, with some reporting retention rates as low as 54% (Caserta & Gillett, 1998) and mainly occurring during the first three months of a programme. This means efforts need to be made to address these risks early on in any intervention. Even after completing a programme, some studies have found that within two years, most interventions to increase exercise in older adults around the age of retirement (55–70 years) had lost their effectiveness. At highest risk of dropout are those who are overweight, on a vigorous physical activity programme, fail to meet their goals early on, are from areas of lower socio-economic status, who are lonely and have low education levels. Taking each of these elements into consideration up front when setting anything up will ensure specific needs are considered.

INTERVENTION IN ACTION: SILVERFIT

Silverfit is a charity designed to promote happier, healthier aging by offering exercise sessions and social activities to those who have retired. They offer 17 activities (such as BMX biking, walking football, Pilates, badminton and cheerleading) in 15 locations in London. The sessions are low cost (£12 a year membership and £0–£3 per session) and involve around an hour of physical activity followed by refreshments in the café. Their research shows their sessions improve quality of life and save health and social care providers money through fewer doctor visits, reduced use of medication and less loneliness.

One of Silverfit's members is 68-year-old Helen. Her story is typical. Before retiring she was so busy with caring for her children and her mother and doing her full-time job that fitting in exercise was really difficult. After retiring she realised how stressed she had been and wanted to try something completely different. Through Silverfit she tried badminton, something she hadn't done since school.

Over the three years she has been attending, she has added activities, grown in confidence and made new friends. "After I stopped work I lost a stone and a half. It came from not snacking and being more active because at work I was really just sitting down all the time at a computer.

"When I first started badminton I couldn't hit the thing but the instructor was so good and helped us take things on. I've definitely learnt a lot. I didn't want to be social – I didn't want to come and drink coffee afterwards – I just wanted to play my game but I suddenly thought my gosh, I've now got all of these people I can now go and play badminton with and I wouldn't have known any of them if I hadn't have had Silverfit.

"At badminton I met the lady who does the Nordic walking. And I joined one of her groups so I learnt Nordic walking that way, so I can just take myself off and that got me into doing a bit more walking which is good. In the future I want to do longer walks. There is a whole heap of places I want to go visit.

"I also do Tai Chi on a Saturday morning. When I started it was a council Adult Education class but they stopped funding it so we turned ourselves into a community group and we've managed to keep going. Tomorrow I'm trying a Pilates class. Without this I feel I could just drift on, and drift is not good. Because you turn round and you'll be 85 and you think 'damn – what did I do with all those retirement years?'

"I do wonder if I would have felt able to do that if I hadn't have had the Silverfit background and getting to know people. I've got friends but they are fairly scattered and it is a whole different scene when you are not working. If you go out to work you've got your work colleagues there and even if it is just 'hi, how are you doing today.' When you stop working you lose your peer group. I think now I am more up for things like exercise since I retired as I realise: 'sod it – what is the worst that could happen.' You've only got one life."

6

PSYCHOLOGY OF EXERCISE WITH A SERIOUS HEALTH CONDITION

Those with health conditions often need far more exercise than they get to build up resilience to their condition, to help them cope better and to improve their quality of life. However, their health condition can change their relationship with exercise and throw up additional barriers and influences on how motivated they are and how much they feel able to do.

To consider the psychology of exercise when facing a health condition, change or crisis here we look at five common health issues: cancer, heart disease, asthma, type 2 diabetes and depression. We will aim to understand the issues, highlight the benefits of exercise to that population, identify the psychological barriers those dealing with the disease might be facing and build up evidence-based best practice for developing programmes to engage this population. We will see how, in addition to the regular barriers that we all face, there are a number of barriers that the actual health condition puts up. Of course, the severity of the symptoms will be different for each person, but if we can understand the main psychological barriers and motivations specific to each condition, we should be able to adapt programmes in the most effective way to increase the amount of exercise completed. This can help secure both physical and mental health benefits. For some, this process is a necessary hardship to go through as part of their recovery. For others it can lead to growth through trauma and help them to develop a new love of physical activity.

PSYCHOLOGY OF EXERCISE WITH CANCER

Exercise is safe and beneficial for cancer survivors. It is linked to better survival and lower recurrence rates, reducing deaths from some cancers by up to 60% (Kenfield, Stampfer, Giovannucci, & Chan, 2011) and disease recurrence by 24% (Ibrahim & Al-Homaidh, 2011). Despite this, few cancer survivors exercise enough. In some studies only 12% of patients (Galvão et al., 2015) have been doing enough exercise even though it is increasingly encouraged to offset the physical side effects, including decreased muscle strength, reduced lean body mass, reduced cardiorespiratory fitness, bone loss and fatigue and the psychological impact of higher anxiety and distress.

The benefits of exercise (ideally both resistance and aerobic exercise) for those dealing with cancer have been found to reduce treatment-related toxicities, improve symptoms, higher fitness levels and fewer hospital stays. Once recovering, it can have a huge number of benefits including improved physical function, better emotional wellbeing, increased muscle strength, higher self-efficacy, better body image, decreased fatigue, anxiety and depression and helps to keep patients at a healthier body weight. Really importantly, physical activity post-cancer treatment has been found to improve quality of life.

Research has found that cancer patients are often aware of these exercise benefits but do not automatically translate this belief into intention or behaviour because they do not believe these benefits outweigh the perceived costs or barriers. This means it is vital for us to understand the costs and barriers.

The biggest barriers for cancer patients come from the side effects of their treatment, such as fatigue, a fear of over-exertion and the actual symptoms associated with the toxicity of anticancer therapeutics, such as pain and vomiting. There is also a fear of making their symptoms worse, and these all combine to create a substantial barrier.

When cancer and the associated treatment has changed someone's physical appearance, there can be a fear of being perceived differently and stigmatised as a victim. This identity elicits sympathy and kindness but reduces the levels of competence the cancer patient is thought to have. When they are seen exercising, the perceived competence levels rise again, and discrimination towards them falls. This changed perception may not just be to other people. They may also internalise these negative beliefs about their physical capabilities and see themselves as weaker and in physical decline.

The final barrier focuses on education, or the lack of it. Patients have reported feeling that their clinicians sometimes have a lack of expertise, time and support infrastructure around exercise. A survey of 460 multi-professional cancer clinicians found lifestyle advice was offered to fewer than 50% of patients (Williams et al., 2010). Along with this lack of general education on the benefits of exercising with cancer, there are also pervading myths which need to be corrected such as the belief that exercise can be harmful when living with cancer.

Together, these 'cancer-driven' barriers can become quite restrictive and go some way to explaining why exercise rates are so low. When they are added onto the day-to-day barriers that all individuals are exposed to, we can understand why their motivation and intention to exercise and then their actual exercise behaviour is so low.

PSYCHOLOGY OF EXERCISE WITH HEART DISEASE

Cardiovascular disease is a leading cause of death, causing 15.9% of all deaths globally (Global Burden of Disease Study, 2015). Once someone has had a heart incident, they may well have reduced exercise capacity, and this can cause a lower quality of life.

Cardiac rehabilitation is recommended as a standard treatment for patients with coronary heart disease recovering from acute events or after surgery. Exercise is a key element of cardiac rehabilitation. When patients follow this treatment, they reduce the negative impacts of the heart disease: decrease mortality risk by 30%, ensure fewer hospital readmissions, reduce risk of recurrent cardiovascular events and lower levels of fatigue. With exercise the coronary risk factor levels (such as obesity, hypertension and elevated blood lipids) fall and the progression of the disease slows.

Cognitively, exercise has been found to help those with heart disease improve their functioning. Mentally it reduces levels of stress and depression, perhaps due to changes in endorphin levels as well as a reduction in the stress hormone cortisol. Individuals who exercise also benefit from greater self-acceptance, positive relations and personal growth from the cardiac incident.

Socially, particularly for young people with heart disease, exercise can not only improve their social functioning but also becomes a normalising endeavour helping them to develop personal and social skills and to feel more on a par with their peers. Taken together these benefits help those with heart disease thrive and improve their quality of life.

Despite these benefits there is poor adherence to regular exercise among people with heart disease, with fewer than half exercising regularly. Many of those who do start on a fitness programme as part of their cardiac rehabilitation fail to maintain these routines over the long term, with dropout rates of up to 50%.

With heart disease there are a huge number of barriers that patients will need to overcome. Many of the environmental issues will be the same for anyone who should be exercising: the cost, the access, the weather conditions, but those with cardiovascular disease will have additional issues of needing to find somewhere to exercise where they feel safe and they could get help if required.

The interpersonal issues they face may also be exacerbated because of their illness. They may not be able to do as much exercise as others, need regular rest breaks and risk reduction policies in place and, if young, may be subject to vulnerable child syndrome where parents overprotect. All of this can result in potentially negative social consequences such as marginalisation or bullying. Where patients do feel like they have higher levels of social support, either through encouragement to be active, by having an exercise companion as they exercise or feeling like they belong in that environment, they exercise more.

Intrapersonal barriers will usually focus on the lack of motivation, interest or time perceived to be available to exercise. The individual's own outcome expectations may also be important here. These will often culminate in their self-efficacy around exercise. Self-efficacy, our measure of our perceived ability, or confidence, to perform a specific behaviour, can be a significant barrier to exercise when low and a great facilitator when high. It can be influenced by peers, by the trust in medical staff and (in young people) by parents. Once someone with heart disease is exercising, if they have the right support and are progressing well, they are likely to grow in both task efficacy (believing they can do specific tasks) and barrier efficacy (believing they can overcome their obstacles). This higher sense of self-efficacy gives patients the competence to initiate intended behaviour change and helps them maintain the behaviour. High self-efficacy, a history of exercise, high intention to exercise, fewer perceived barriers and lots of self-regulation ensure much higher exercise levels.

The disease itself will also create a significant barrier to exercise. The cardiovascular disease factors such as breathlessness and exhaustion, poor physical condition, lethargy, reduced energy levels and reduced exercise capacity, particularly after surgery and with low previous physical activity levels, will all act as an initial barrier. Beyond this there will also be a perception barrier with feelings of physical restriction and becoming fearful of exercise, particularly the fatigue which it may cause.

A final and extensive barrier worthy of focus is the high level of depression found in cardiac patients, with some studies finding as many as 36% of men and 62% of women suffer from it within six months of a cardiac admission, up to three times as high as in the general population (Ali, Stone, Peters, Davies, & Khunti, 2006). Depression is a risk factor for increased morbidity and mortality for those with cardiovascular disease and can also bring with it social isolation, anxiety and hostility, all of which have been linked with higher mortality and morbidity in cardiac patients.

For many, structured exercise can decrease depressive symptoms and has been found to be as effective as anti-depression medication or Cognitive Behavioural Therapy, resulting in improved survival levels. However, depressive symptoms represent a major barrier to exercise behaviour change in those with cardiovascular disease, and even those exercising are often not doing enough to benefit as the depression itself can exacerbate non-adherence to exercise, the low mood it causes and the negative perceptions of their health it prompts, meaning it becomes a barrier to taking positive action and initiating or maintaining an exercise habit.

The level of depression can also inhibit a patient's sense of purpose. This is important because having a reason for exercising, even an extrinsic one like doing the exercise for someone other than themselves, can be a major motivation. This purpose can be for their children, an obligation to health professionals or to feel like they are getting their health back, but when they have it, it becomes an important facilitator to exercise and one worth health professionals promoting in their work with these individuals.

PSYCHOLOGY OF EXERCISE WITH ASTHMA

Asthma, a chronic respiratory disease involving hyper-responsiveness in the airways, inflammation and airflow obstruction is common, affecting an estimated 300 million people worldwide (Braman, 2006). Prevalence rates are said to be around 8–15%, and asthma accounts for more than 25% of all school absences (Mallol et al., 2013; Lenfant & Hurd, 1990).

It is a serious condition but is not always taken seriously, even by those suffering from it. Only 70% of prescriptions for asthma medication in an Australian study were even taken to the pharmacy to be collected (Watts, McLennan, Bassham, & El-Saadi, 1997), and only around 35% of children and 50% of adults are using their medication as they should (Davis, Disantostefano, & Peden, 2011; Bender, Milgrom, & Apter, 2003) suggesting that fewer than half of asthma sufferers are controlling their condition effectively.

There are a number of triggers for asthma, including environmental irritants or allergens (such as tobacco smoke), cold air, viral infection, exercise, stress and anxiety. To control their asthma those suffering from it need to manage these triggers and take preventative medication. As exercise is one of the most common triggers of asthma symptoms, with up to 80% of asthmatics suffering from exercise-induced asthma (McFadden & Gilbert, 1994), it is not surprising that asthmatics have low rates of physical activity. Studies have found that more than half of asthmatics purposely try to avoid exertion (Davis et al., 2011), leaving them with a relatively sedentary lifestyle. Once this attitude has taken hold, it is hard to overcome as they not only have to address their fear of health risks but can also perceive themselves to be less fit or competent and so feel embarrassed and unsure if where to start.

Exercise avoidance through a sedentary lifestyle will feel safe, but it is unhealthy. A number of studies have found that physical activity has a really positive long-term impact on those with asthma, improving cardiopulmonary fitness, general health, sleep, asthma symptoms, lung function, coping behaviours for asthma and their overall quality of life. This means the 'safe option' of avoiding exercise may actually physically exacerbate their asthma long term and socially isolate them from peers, harming their self-confidence, emotional wellbeing and development.

Another trigger is emotional stress and anxiety. Evidence links emotional distress to greater asthma severity, worse asthma control and increased use of emergency and general health services. This is a really difficult trigger to control as asthmatics have been found to have higher levels of depression, anxiety and obesity, which all contribute to poorer asthma control and more symptoms.

The depression and anxiety can see us becoming less physically active, contributing to weight gain and reduced asthma control.

Together these can reduce self-efficacy, so asthmatics may not believe they can control their asthma, meaning they are even less likely to exercise, become more negatively impacted by stress, have poorer stress-coping processes and ultimately worse health outcomes. Physical activity is a really effective tool to help reduce stress, anxiety and depressive symptoms, but the symptoms which come with all of these health conditions can also act as a barrier to exercise. Improving the self-efficacy of asthmatics around exercise would boost their confidence so that they can cope with their asthma, increase their compliance to medication, reduce hospitalisation rates and improve their asthma-related quality of life.

When asthmatics don't exercise through low levels of asthma self-efficacy, from the fear of having an asthma attack or having to overcome the barriers put up by their mental health or obesity, then there can be a considerable impact on their daily quality of life. When children don't manage their asthma properly, there is not just a heavy personal risk to their health and physical functioning, but they also risk having psychosocial maladjustment and may feel like a burden on their parents, school systems, communities, health care providers and the entire health care system.

Health professionals say that as long as there is the right support in place, there should be no difference in the levels of exercise that can be achieved by asthmatics. This means it is really important that exercise is incorporated into the lives of asthmatics, even though there will be some specific barriers to overcome, both physically and psychologically.

One of the biggest barriers comes from the fear of having an asthma attack as a result of exercise. When this happens, it can be incredibly scary. Overcoming that fear to continue to exercise requires support. Education could help asthmatics overcome some of these fears, but it can be hard to come by as it can be restricted by health care staff not having the time to promote physical activity as their initial focus needs to be on symptom control and medicinal aspects. The education an asthmatic has had around their condition may influence their perception of themselves, their potential abilities and their illness belief system. It can also influence how they perceive their physiological feelings and whether they see something like shortness of breath as an asthma symptom requiring them to stop exercising or just an outcome of exercise that happens to everyone.

Parents of asthmatic children could help with this; however, studies have found they often become overprotective around exercise, and instead of encouraging it, actually set limits.

PSYCHOLOGY OF EXERCISE WITH TYPE 2 DIABETES MELLITUS (T2DM)

Type 2 diabetes mellitus (T2DM) has become a global epidemic, with many countries projecting that up to 10% of their population currently or will soon suffer from it (Australia; Baker, 2012; USA; Centers for Disease Control, 2018). Worldwide over 420 million people are currently living with diabetes (WHO, 2018a).

While T2DM has an obvious impact on physical health, it has a hidden but clear impact on mental health too. Forty percent of sufferers have symptoms of anxiety, and 30% have symptoms of depression (Grigsby, Anderson, Freedland, Clouse, & Lustman, 2002; Ali et al., 2006); prevalence rates nearly double the rates found in the general population and cause poor quality of life. The depressive symptoms can then link to poor glycaemic control, more health complications and higher mortality rates.

Exercise is a critical component of the effective self-management of T2DM in reducing both the symptoms and severity and has become a key route to improving quality of life. Both physical exertion and resistance training can help with the physical symptoms associated with T2DM by enhancing insulin sensitivity, improving blood glucose control, producing helpful changes in body composition and having positive effects on blood pressure and HDL cholesterol. It has also been found to help reduce glycated haemoglobin levels, irrespective of whether there is an improvement in cardiorespiratory fitness.

There is also a strong wellbeing benefit for exercise for those with T2DM as it can help alleviate the fatigue-related symptoms, increase and improve the amount and quality of sleep and generally improve psychological wellbeing. Specifically, around depression, studies have found that even low amounts of physical activity can make a positive difference to the number of depressive symptoms felt. Despite this, a huge proportion of people who have already developed T2DM remain inactive, with fewer than a quarter of diabetic adults in the UK meeting government physical activity recommendations and a high proportion struggling to maintain a healthy weight.

There are a number of specific barriers which are related to the diabetes, the side effects of it and its symptoms, which means those with diabetes will have more barriers to confront than other adults. First off, exercise can be particularly uncomfortable when you are overweight, which many people with type 2 diabetes are. Those individuals will complain they are too heavy to exercise, they dislike sweating and it causes them pain and physical discomfort. Other health problems which come from T2DM and create barriers include a general poor state of health, bad feet, a lack of energy to exercise and feeling too sleepy or fatigued to exercise. The prevalence of depression, which can also be much higher in those with T2DM, can also behave as a barrier as can a fear of making their physical condition worse.

The final barrier from the implications of already having a serious health condition is that sometimes these patients do not know what they should be doing, feel left in the dark and find there is no supervision to support any attempts at exercise, so it becomes easier not to do it. These feelings are supported by a study of health professionals who say while they are committed to promoting physical activity to adults with diabetes, in practice they often lack education and training around physical activity so can be unaware of guidelines, referral options and specialised resources.

There are also internal barriers raised by patients which are influenced by the individual's own decision-making. They include lack of time, willpower and motivation, laziness and just not seeing exercise as a priority. In one study, 40% of patients admitted they were simply unmotivated to exercise (Alharbi et al., 2017). These will be similar issues and barriers that may have caused them to develop T2DM in the first place so will be deeply ingrained into their mindset towards exercise. We see this when participants in studies claim they have a lack of time to exercise yet also have enough free time to watch significant amounts of television.

Three key areas can be seen to proactively influence the amount of physical activity completed by those with T2DM: how they feel doing it (the effect), their level of self-efficacy and the support they have around them.

The effect of exercise upon us, how it makes us feel has a strong influence and impacts our decision-making extensively. If we enjoy exercising, we will do more of it. Even if we don't enjoy it at the time but we enjoy how it makes us feel afterwards, that is effective too. For those who need to adopt a healthier lifestyle, self-efficacy will be important because it predicts their persistence with a new behaviour and how much effort they are likely to put in. The stronger a diabetic's self-efficacy the more effective they are likely to be at incorporating exercise into their lives. Finally, social support is key with numerous studies highlighting positive relationships between exercise levels and social and family support, social engagement and the relationships and interactions which come during and around exercise. In particular is the element of encouragement and wanting to emulate others in our social circle who are active, so role modelling can be really effective.

PSYCHOLOGY OF EXERCISE WITH DEPRESSION

Depression is a chronic condition suffered by over 264 million people worldwide (GBD Collaborators, 2017), and it is one of the largest sources of disability and disease burden. It is more common among women than men, with female/male risk ratios of about 2:1. Depression can have a strong and negative impact on an individual's mental and physical health, which can lead to reduced quality of life and lower life expectancy. Depression also influences our risk of developing a number of other chronic physical health conditions such as type 2 diabetes, coronary heart disease and obesity. Fewer than half of patients taking anti-depressants in an adequate dose experience a meaningful clinical response, and so alternative approaches for treating depression are essential. Exercise is one of these alternative approaches.

Firstly, exercise can help prevent depression in the first place. A study found that 12% of new cases could be prevented if the whole population exercised for at least one hour per week as regular exercisers are less likely to develop emotional disorders (Harvey, Øverland, Hatch et al., 2018).

If depression has already been diagnosed, then exercise has been found to be an effective way to prevent and reduce depressive symptoms for both severe and mild depression. It is now a recommended treatment and has been found to be as effective as taking anti-depressants, decreasing depressive symptoms by as much as 70% (Blumenthal et al., 2007).

Both cardiovascular and resistance exercise, either independently or combined, have been found to be beneficial, with more frequent exercise being significantly associated with fewer or less severe symptoms of depression and improved quality of life. The impact can be quick, with a reduction in symptoms being seen even after just six weeks, but it does need to be continued to ensure long-term improvement.

There are a number of theories as to why exercise has a positive impact connecting the complex interactions between neurobiological, physical, cognitive and psychosocial factors. Cognitively exercise provides us with structure, purpose, energy and motivation in other areas of life. It also alters the way we process and respond to our emotions, reduces our rumination and builds our emotional resilience to stress. Psycho-socially exercise in groups can induce feelings of social inclusion and connectedness to nature and other people. It can help us develop a greater sense of engagement in life and the immediate situation, moving towards a more activated, outward-focused state. For our wider wellbeing a key benefit is the positive emotion exercise induces. It can increase pleasure, improve mood, self-esteem and self-worth to create a general feel-better effect all while reducing anxiety and distressing emotions. Exercise is also relatively inexpensive, can suit those who are concerned about taking medication, improves cardiovascular functioning and avoids potential medication side effects.

The benefits are recognised not just by health care professionals but by those with the conditions themselves. Many people with depression are aware and sold on the idea that physical activity can help to reduce their depressive symptoms, and yet those with depression do less exercise than others, are less likely to follow exercise recommendations and, even when they are placed into trials investigating the effect of exercise on symptoms of depression, adherence rates have been found to be as low as 50% (Callaghan, Khalil, Morres, & Carter, 2011).

Those with depression say the primary barrier to participation in physical activities is their own mental health. Their poor mental health results in a vicious circle: depression leads to a reduction in exercise, and a reduction in exercise aggravates depression. When you are in this cycle, you find it more difficult to alter, upregulate or stabilise your mood after it has declined, and so you become stuck in a negative mood state, heightening your risk for depression onset, maintenance and relapse. Depressed individuals may also have a motivational deficit, being less capable of transforming their intentions into actions, so they are less likely to produce action plans, have lower self-efficacy, expect negative outcomes and are susceptible to barrier distraction. Coping planning would help to keep these people on track and bat away any barriers more effectively, but depression can prevent them from planning effectively for the future.

An additional barrier is that depressed individuals can interpret situations and social interactions in a manner that is consistent with their own perception of themselves, so everything can feel bleak. The filter through which life can be seen when you are dealing with depression can significantly impact a person's beliefs about their capabilities. They may become unable to accept the truth, reality or validity about their ability or capability to learn. The generalised confidence that others might use to try and overcome these fears is missing. When exercise is also connected to having to interact with others, this fear and lack of confidence can become overwhelming. The low self-efficacy this causes translates into their exercise intentions. When you are unsure of what you want in your own future, or even if you want a future, future proofing your health by exercising feels pointless.

When exercise is undertaken though, it can not only reduce some of the depressive symptoms but also improve functional health and quality of life as well as improve symptoms from any other co-morbid serious health conditions, again reducing the impact of depression. Many of these conditions (such as asthma, obesity and cardiovascular disease) will contribute towards physical inactivity and a loss of fitness, and people with symptoms of depression often report physical fatigue and a lack of motivation, so this can become a really negative cycle to escape.

Health behaviour change is more challenging for those with a mental health issue than the general population. For example, the physical barriers that many people confront (a lack of energy or being too tired or lethargic) can become amplified with depression. These barriers feel like walls as those with depression cite more than three barriers that interfere with their exercise attempts, and the more depressive symptoms they have the more barriers they perceive are stopping them from exercising.

When the depressed person does do some exercise and is able to see how it increases their self-esteem, expands their social support and engagement systems, distracts from negative thoughts, offers genuine enjoyment in the feeling of the movement or provides a sense of engagement in life, it can behave as a facilitator. When these positive physical activity experiences lead them to knowing exercise makes them feel good and improves their situation, it can become self-reinforcing, facilitating more exercise taking place. With this they move from a level of extrinsic motivation to one which is much more intrinsic. This change in motivation helps them overcome barriers to being active, and some begin to use physical activity to self-manage symptoms.

DESIGNING EXERCISE PROGRAMMES FOR THOSE WITH A HEALTH CONDITION

Successful programmes for those with a health condition often combine a number of models and theories. They allow for development of competency, autonomy and community, promote the growth of self-efficacy and support people at all stages along the process. In this way they can ensure that the mechanisms of sustained behaviour change are in place to facilitate long-term and effective exercise habits. This should reduce the negative impacts of living with one of these health conditions and start to make the barriers feel more negotiable.

MYTH-BUSTING EDUCATION

Many of the physical or health barriers caused by different health conditions can be overcome with relevant education. Those who have gone through an education programme about their condition with a specialist find they improve their relevant knowledge, exercise more and improve their quality of life. As exercise can feel like a risk when one is dealing with a health condition, confronting each of the potential barriers – both the barriers we all have (like lack of motivation or our abilities to control our behaviours) and those specific to that health condition (such as exercising increasing fatigue) – can be handled effectively through education. The same is true of the benefits that exercise could offer them. When the individual benefits of exercise for each health condition are explained, the individual becomes reassured about how much is possible, and more are empowered to engage. Very specific elements, such as helping people to learn the difference between exercise-induced breathlessness and specific symptoms of the health conditions or how and when to avoid triggers, may also help to reduce some of the fear.

It is important that any education is part of a wider process though. Offering tailored information (videos, pamphlets or guidelines) alone is seen as ineffective. Effective approaches need to be systematic and centred on the individual. A cost-effective way to do this can be through small-group educational programmes as they combine knowledge delivery, a supportive forum and peer engagement. This then goes beyond information and helps people facilitate, integrate and internalise exercise behaviour. This is what makes them not just start exercising but stick with it. But education alone does not go far enough. It also needs to be communicated in the right way. Exercise levels increase when knowledge about exercise and its benefits is delivered in a counselling manner where the personal barriers and constraints of the individual are clearly recognised and taken into account and when it is used to show how others in similar situations have adapted.

MOTIVATIONAL SUPPORT

One of the key predictors of exercise behaviour is the support an individual has in doing it, ideally from both experts and their friends or family. Support should be brief but regular. Initially the focus is on helping people to identify their barriers and then developing solutions so they are able to overcome them so they can focus more strongly on the benefits and on their specific motivators. Once this is in place, there should be regular check-ins to encourage individuals to identify their main reasons for exercise as this enhances their focus and helps them engage in a continual goal-setting process. Slowly developing the exercise programmes, reinforcing goal completion and monitoring energy levels after exercise can all help individuals overcome some of the barriers put up by their health condition.

Coming either from the person running the programme or an outside counsellor, motivational interviewing that focuses on identifying and reducing barriers to exercise has been found to be really effective. These regular check-ins increase the amount of exercise which takes place by developing a supportive atmosphere where the individual still feels autonomous. It means they can develop their own source of motivation to set goals which are personally meaningful and create action plans which focus on overcoming their specific barriers while fitting into their own life circumstances. Emphasising the importance of finding exercise which feels enjoyable is key to develop continuous exercise maintenance. The more barriers, and the more health side effects the condition causes, the more support and reassurance is required from professionals.

Ideally the support comes from a multi-disciplinary team (such as physicians, nurses, pharmacists, physiotherapists, health educators and fitness experts) with the patient at the centre. From this, a consistent, evidence-based, joined-up approach tends to occur, so the individual benefits from exercise in all areas of their condition. The presence of so many experts not only gives reassurance but also ensures medical history and previous exercise is taken into account. To ensure individuals remain exercising even after official programmes have completed, support can also be valuable to help people transition out of a 'health condition' exercise programme into habitual exercise which is incorporated into their life.

PERSONALISED PROGRAMMES

There are some fundamental elements of the physical design of a programme for those with a health condition that are helpful to increase positive outcomes. What has been found to be effective for most health conditions is a protocol of a programme of at least 30 minutes duration, undertaken at least three times a week that incorporates both cardiovascular exercise and resistance exercise for at least nine weeks.

Beyond these parameters it has been found that person-centred, behavioural approaches improve the chances of achieving the desired exercise outcomes. The number of barriers involved and restrictions that come from the health condition mean that programmes for this group need extensive personalisation tailored to the individual's health condition, previous experience, individual aims and motivations and fitness level.

Once the barriers have been assessed and acknowledged, programmes can be designed and advice and guidance offered that can counter them. Some of this information can be computer generated to be more cost effective, but the customisation to the specific barriers that the health condition causes has been found to be essential.

Practically, the impact of any medication on physical activities also needs to be accounted or adjusted for, and the impact of the condition itself on their health and physiology is considered, not just due to physical barriers or the fear or exacerbating symptoms but psychological ones too, whether these are around embarrassment or the lack of motivation or self-efficacy, which can come from having a health condition.

In addition to meeting the needs of the health condition, personalisation works because adherence is highest when exercise is enjoyed, is self-paced and completed at the individual's preferred intensity. Having a choice of a wide range of exercise options can increase the chances of an individual finding one which they enjoy. The more a physical activity is a positive experience the sooner the individual can see and reflect upon the positive benefits and will begin to shift towards intrinsic motivation for exercising.

Once someone has become aware of and experienced the general psychological changes that come from exercise – the relaxation, being able to think through problems or stresses or enhancing their sense of achievement and the personal benefits highlighted in their own programme – it can act as an important facilitator in them maintaining their exercise levels as they have internalised those exercise behaviours and routines into their lives.

IMPROVING SELF-EFFICACY

As we saw in Chapter 1, self-efficacy is the strongest and most consistent predictor of both aerobic physical activity and resistance training. It is resilient and determines effort, persistence and performance when we exercise.

Studies have found that self-efficacy works most effectively when alongside autonomous motivation. It gives people the drive to make changes and the belief they can stick with the new behaviours. There are a number of ways we can proactively help someone increase their self-efficacy, and doing this early in any programme is important as it means they are more likely to make the effort to start exercising and more likely to persist at overcoming their specific barriers that they face along the way.

An element which will boost a patient's self-efficacy is their knowledge about their disease and how exercise can be beneficial. When there is a knowledge gap, it can act as a barrier. When they become educated as to the benefits of exercise and the correct type, amount and intensity required for people with their issues, they will feel more confident to take on more. As the patient starts to see the benefits of the exercise and reflects on the journey they have been on to start exercising and making health behaviour changes, they can go through a process of meaning making and find it has been of benefit.

After that educational process, a goal should be set. Ideally the goal will be a behavioural one (rather than outcome based), short term and easy to reach. Then some training in cognitive restructuring can help to turn negative outcome expectations into thoughts which more effectively enhance feelings of self-efficacy. Finally, setting up the exercise environment for individuals to develop mastery so they improve their confidence in their physical ability alongside actually improving their abilities helps to build confidence and makes the process of exercise more appealing. When we add in the education around what is possible and achievable for those with their health condition, social support from others with a similar condition and vicarious experience (in the form of role models), then self-efficacy can grow and exercise becomes more compelling and easier to engage with.

DEVELOPING THE ABILITY TO SELF-REGULATE

However well planned and neatly designed an exercise intervention is it will always be time limited. The real success is when participants have built up their self-efficacy to want to continue once the formal support has been withdrawn. They can do this if they have developed skills and learnt tools for behavioural self-regulation. Behaviour change programmes grounded in self-regulation theory have been found to have longer-lasting effects, and the specific skills used to overcome and then reduce the barriers along the way become valuable tools to self-regulate exercise long term.

One such regularly used technique is tracking. Tracking exercise can encourage the maintenance of exercise and can strengthen motivation. Tools used for tracking include self-monitoring equipment (such as pedometers or fitness trackers), feedback notification (constantly recording current activity), reminders to be active, self-help workbooks and keeping an exercise diary. Beyond tracking, wider cognitive behavioural strategies such as goal setting, feedback to improve exercise adherence, anticipation of personal barriers, and the development of coping planning have all been found to be effective.

When we pull many of these techniques together, we get 'action planning.' It can help individuals develop a plan for when and where to engage in exercise, as well as how to overcome potential barriers. It becomes necessary for the maintenance of exercise after someone has been doing it for a while to make it more sustainable and is particularly helpful for those with depression (which may come with many of the health conditions discussed here) as they may lack concrete plans for action.

These action plans should help individuals as they move through the distinct phases of behavioural change: initial response, continued response, maintenance and habit. The planning process can take into account the different types of support, motivational prompts and tools required at each stage, ensuring the personalisation around their own barriers and motivators, the limitations imposed by their health condition and that the support offered matches the individual's needs.

INTERVENTION IN ACTION: 5K YOUR WAY, MOVE AGAINST CANCER

As a former professional athlete, consultant oncologist Lucy Gossage is passionate about the benefits of exercise, particularly so when living with a health condition. "There is a growing body of evidence that exercise is beneficial for patients living with cancer. It reduces fatigue and depression, improves health related quality of life and there is now evolving evidence that it impacts on tumour biology too. It's early evidence but it's likely that physical activity has a positive impact on treatment outcomes and survival."

Exercise isn't just about recovery though. Prehabilitation is also helpful, says Gossage. "There is evidence now about the benefits of pre-operative optimisation before surgery, basically getting fit for surgery. The operations cancer patients need can have enormous physiological demands, and chemotherapy courses can also be very intensive. Incorporating physical activity into Prehabilitation programmes as part of standard cancer care will be really beneficial."

In June 2018 Gossage treated a patient with a rare brain tumour. Despite the treatment being successful, this young man had put on enormous amounts of weight and felt that through cancer he had lost everything he had going for him, including his job and his friends. Gossage realised they should be doing more to support people when they finish treatment and thought exercise in a group setting would provide both physical and psychological benefits.

Along with Gemma Hilier-Moses, Gossage set up 5k Your Way, Move Against Cancer, an active support group with a difference which encourages those living with and beyond cancer, families, friends and those working in cancer services to walk, jog, run, cheer or volunteer at a local 5k Your Way group within designated parkruns on the last Saturday of every month. They started the first group in Nottingham and within 18 months expanded to 58 venues around the UK. "Jumping on the back of parkrun is brilliant as parkrun is, I think, one of the most successful public health initiatives in the world. Creating a community within a community is really powerful and it means outside of 5k your way there is somewhere for people to go independently – it can catapult them to try something new.

"Until recently, the general advice from health care professionals to patients was to rest. We now know this isn't what is best for most patients and little by little, we are becoming more pro-active about encouraging patients to move more. I think one of the biggest barriers from the patients' perceptive is that their loved ones often want to wrap cotton wool round them and protect them. We need to give people permission to be active and stay active. We need them to know that one of the biggest things you can do for your cancer outcome is to stay active. Not just that you can be active but that it is good to be active."

The feedback from people who attend 5k Your Way, Move Against Cancer groups is really positive. Having a monthly goal to do something positive amongst others in similar situations is powerful. Exercise can give people back a sense of control over their body, something cancer often takes away, and the benefits of a peer support network are enormous. "Many of our 5k Your Wayers feel they are doing something positive by exercising and being in the fresh air and being with others," says Gossage. "Most of the time they are not even talking about cancer but to be with others who get it and know what they are feeling is really powerful. And if they're not feeling up to walking or running, they can still get similar feelings by volunteering and joining the group for a drink afterwards."

7

THE PSYCHOLOGY OF EXERCISE ADDICTION

Every chapter in this book has highlighted the immense benefits which stem from engaging in regular exercise: reducing the risk of a host of both acute and chronic physical and mental health issues and positively influencing cognitive performance and wellbeing. On occasion though, the motivation which is often lacking in those not exercising enough is found in abundance in those who are exercising so much that it has become harmful to their health. This is known as exercise addiction.

Addictive behaviours, where an individual tries to escape real life by artificially changing their physical or mental state (through something like gaming or exercise) can often start out as beneficial to the individual but over time progresses until it is pathologically excessive. This is particularly obvious in exercise addiction where the physical effort and energy expenditure required for exercise can initially benefit their mental and physical health, but when its use turns into an obsessive and unhealthy preoccupation, then a disorder arises. The disorder is part of a continuum developing in stages, progressing from healthy to unhealthy as the individual uses exercise to modify their mood and requires increasingly higher doses in order to get their 'fix.'

Someone suffering from exercise addiction will be increasing their time or intensity exercising and, even if following specific training plans, they may add extra repetitions or minutes to their sessions. They will devote more and more time to exercise, making friends at classes or clubs and even taking fitness-related holidays so that they have a reason to continue. As they become preoccupied by exercise, it embeds as a key part of their identity. Non-fitness activities tend to feel like a nuisance or fall by the wayside.

Over time the individual will adopt meticulous and inflexible behaviours, so they feel unable to reduce intensity, frequency or time committed to exercise. They will become frustrated and angry at the thought of missing a session and suffer severe withdrawal symptoms if they cannot exercise. If they try to stop, they report higher levels of depression, confusion, anger, fatigue, an inability to sleep and concentrate, restlessness, anxiety, sadness or irritability. Even just one day of exercise deprivation can increase tension and depressed mood, and so they often relapse.

Once this is in place, the person finds that exercise has become all-consuming and can suffer damaging effects such as fatigue and injury, personal inconvenience, marital strain, interference with work or reduced time for other activities. They can also suffer from lower self-satisfaction, poor social behaviour and reduced vigour, and exercise starts to form the basis of most of their conflicts. And despite all these negative effects, they will continue to exercise.

This final element is what separates obsessive or high levels of exercise from addiction, the conflict that exercise causes. A young person with few responsibilities, lots of free time and a fairly robust body could do 20 hours of exercise a week, and we wouldn't consider them to be addicted. But the same level of exercise in a person who has a job, young children and parental caring responsibilities may find their exercise habits causing regular conflict and relationship angst and would be considered to have moved into the addicted arena.

MODELS OF EXERCISE ADDICTION

A number of models have been created suggesting how and why exercise addiction arises. Many of the psychological approaches towards the development of addictions come from the behaviourist perspective where actions are either positively or negatively reinforced. Here exercise can be seen as a positive reinforcer as increased training, effort and focus usually improve the individual's performance over time. In triathletes it was found that, after exercise, they experience increases in perceived efficacy (like mastery, competence and control) which all become positive reinforcers. With Skinner (1989) proposing that reinforcement is superior to punishment in altering behaviour, it may be that any detrimental effect of over-exercising (discomfort, injury, lack of time) would be less of a deterrent than the motivation which comes from the positive reinforcement of the behaviour.

An interactional model (Egorov & Szabo, 2013) could also account for the adoption, maintenance and transformation of exercising as it highlights how unique characteristics of individuals interact when there is a need to cope with stressful life events. The interactional model suggests that there are many personal values, social images, past exercise experiences and life situations which can cause someone to use exercise as a way of dealing with stress. There may be a specific situation or stressor over which the person feels no control which triggers their coping mechanism of exercise. With enough of these stressors in place, exercise may become compulsive. This links with the findings in a number of studies that those at risk from exercise addiction tend to also suffer from difficulties in other areas in their lives (Warner & Griffiths, 2006), which could explain why exercise addiction emerges suddenly and only in a few individuals from among those at high risk.

A psychophysiological model (focused on how our thoughts, feelings and behaviours impact on our physiological processes) has come about from studying how brain activity has been related to affect and mood. Brain scans of those with exercise addiction suggest there is greater activity at right frontal sites in the brain among individuals suffering from negative affect and depression, exactly what we would expect to see, as, often in those who are addicted, exercise is used to control negative mood states.

There are also a number of biological models. Some of these are based on the links between exercise addiction and eating disorders, and others focus on the reward systems. Reward system models suggest that the central effects of endorphins in creating the sensation of euphoria that can be felt after exercise is responsible for whether or not dependences or addictive behaviours appear, and craving this is what may lead to exercise addiction. There is also a thermogenic regulation hypothesis which argues that exercising can act as a positive reinforcement because it increases our body temperature which reduces anxiety and increases relaxation. Finally, a biopsychosocial model has been considered as those with exercise addiction were found to hold more extreme and maladaptive exercise beliefs, felt higher pressure from coaches and teammates and perceived they had lower levels of social support.

RISK FACTORS

The range of possible models for exercise addiction shows there is still work to be done to identify the causes, yet there are a number of risk factors that indicate potential predispositions to exercise addiction. These have mainly focused on personality traits, social influences, disordered eating, obsessive compulsiveness, the type of sport involved, appearance anxiety and some individual factors.

Personality traits found to be indicative of a higher risk of exercise addiction have been high levels of narcissism, extroversion, conscientiousness, excitement-seeking, perfectionism, neuroticism and achievement striving and low levels of agreeableness. Research has suggested that exaggerated exercise is linked to obsessive compulsiveness due to difficulty in defining the correct or appropriate levels of exercise, and excessive exercisers do rate higher on obsessive-compulsive symptomatology than non-excessive exercisers.

There is also a greater occurrence of exercise addiction in those who are involved in image-focused recreational or professional activities and in students studying a sport-related degree. We can see this clearly when we look at prevalence levels. While there is a huge amount of inconsistency within reported prevalence rates due to the incomplete conceptual models of exercise addiction, we can see that across the general public exercise addiction rates are very low at around 0.5% (Monok et al., 2012). Those working or interacting regularly in an exercise environment, such as sports science students, have been found to have a risk of addiction between 6.9% and 14.9% (Szabo & Griffiths, 2007; Sicilia, Alias-Garcia, Ferriz, & Moreno-Murcia, 2013). Those competing in endurance sports have much higher risk levels found to be around 20% in triathletes, 27% in runners and up to 44.7% in ultra-endurance athletes (Youngman & Simpson, 2014; Scheer & Hahn, 2014; Perry, 2018).

Elements from the type of exercise itself may also play some part in their addiction. In triathlon it was found the longer the race distance the higher the risk of addiction and, as the number of weekly training hours increased, so did an athlete's risk of addiction. When distance runners were researched, it was their levels of competitiveness which differentiated their risk of exercise addiction with the more competitive runners at highest risk. There are also a number of individual factors which come into play, suggesting the risk gets higher as we age and can be impacted by the environment in which we exercise.

The final risk factor, and one which needs careful consideration, is having an eating disorder. The entwining of exercise addiction with disordered eating is so strong that there are now seen to be two types of exercise addiction: primary and secondary. While exercise addiction can be a primary condition which is driven solely by the psychological gratification which comes from the exercise, it can also co-occur with an eating disorder where the exercise is used as a way to control weight. When it co-occurs it becomes known as secondary exercise addiction. This group is significant as those with eating disorders are over 3.5 times more likely to suffer from addiction to exercise than others (Trott et al., 2020), with prevalence rates in those with eating disorders ranging from 29% to 80% (Dalle Grave, Calugi, & Marchesini, 2008; Bratland-Sanda et al., 2011).

What tends to amplify these risks is that excessive exercise is not only socially accepted but openly celebrated where it can be seen as a 'badge of honour' to show you are working hard and that you are dedicated and driven towards achieving your goal. This can mask the risk factors and hide the cases where exercise addiction is causing real harm and conflict.

TREATMENT FOR EXERCISE ADDICTION

A fully evidence-based treatment protocol for those with an exercise addiction has not yet been established. In cases of secondary exercise addiction, treatment will be driven by the eating disorder as this is a more serious condition and exercise may be completely stopped.

Where someone is suffering from primary exercise addiction, the goal of a programme would not be to prevent them from exercising at all but to help them recognise the addictive behaviour and reduce exercise routine rigidity.

The programme would begin with education and self-awareness. In the first stages, those with exercise addiction would probably find it beneficial to work jointly with fitness professionals and psychologists to develop an appropriate and safe training programme and to re-learn how to use internal sensations, such as pain and fatigue, so they can differentiate between appropriate and excessive training. Then they should work to distinguish between healthy and unhealthy motivators and to reduce ways they can compare themselves with others.

Early on in recovery the person is likely to be suffering from withdrawal symptoms, which would include symptoms of depression, confusion, anger and fatigue. Education will be vital to explain why these are occurring, and support needs to be in place to help the person through this period.

Some of this work can be completed through an approach called Motivational Interviewing, where a therapist or counsellor uses a guiding style to engage people so they can clarify their strengths and aspirations, develop their own motivations for change and feel really autonomous in their decision-making. Another route that is often taken though is Cognitive Behavioural Therapy (CBT). This approach helps the person to restructure maladaptive beliefs about exercise and manage the mood, emotional and cognitive disturbances that have fuelled the addiction.

A specific version of CBT which has gained some traction in those with exercise addiction is Rational Emotive Behaviour Therapy (REBT; Ellis, 1957). REBT suggests that all disturbance occurs as a consequence of dysfunctional information processing. In changing irrational beliefs through cognitive restructuring and promoting rational beliefs, it says we should be able to improve psychological health and wellbeing. In the case of exercise addiction, the irrational beliefs are likely to be around the impact of missing an exercise session. The resulting emotions like anxiety or guilt can be questioned to reduce rigid or harmful behaviours. In an REBT programme for three gym users, it was found that six 45-minute one-to-one counselling sessions and five homework assignments could effectively reduce both the irrational beliefs and the exercise addiction symptoms (Outar, Turner, Wood, & Lowry, 2018).

The interesting point to note is that the interventions which are being tried for those with exercise addiction, CBT, Motivational Interviewing, psycho-education and self-awareness are those which also work well for those attempting to start and maintain an exercise habit. The models and theories which explain why someone might hold back from exercising can often, when flipped around, clearly show why someone might also be over-exercising. These two groups are not at opposite ends of a spectrum. When something requires physical effort, discomfort and time to be executed well and is influenced by our personal preferences, personality traits, upbringing, previous and current environment, logistical and physical barriers and facilitators and our physical and mental health, then the process is neither smooth nor simple. The journey will be up and down, and the lessons learnt along the way valuable to pack into our tool kit to incorporate exercise into our lives in a healthy and enjoyable way.

INTERVENTION IN ACTION: MARIANNE

When Marianne decided to use running as a way to cope with pressures she was facing in life, it proved incredibly effective. "I was overloaded with work and university deadlines and so I'd get up really early in the morning before the children were awake and go out running. I loved that it was just me and I had the freedom and control for my running legs to take me wherever my head wanted to go. The endorphin high was addictive. I craved that post-run high. I came back from a run feeling on top of the world, buzzing and alive like nothing could stop me. But that frenzied feeling only pushed me to do more and more. It also made me anxious to plan my next run and when anything got in the way of that, my anxiety levels rose and that feeling of being out of control re-surged. I was stuck in a really difficult cycle, and the only option was to keep going round and round. I really feared what might happen if I suddenly stopped."

Like many others with exercise addiction, it was injury that forced her to face up to the issue. She developed a stress fracture in her pelvis and some damage to her pubic bone, most likely caused by excessive running. "When I got injured I was utterly lost. It hit me like a sledgehammer. At the time I was so dependent, it was like the rug had been pulled from under my feet. I hated my body for letting me down and I hated running for taking away one of the things I relied on most. All the mental pain I'd been trying to hide from engulfed me."

While difficult at the time, the injury forced her to address the underlying issues that had meant she over-exercised. "Getting injured stopped me in my tracks and forced me to get help. Initially the help was physical, my body needed to rest. I had stretched myself in every possible direction dealing with some really big personal and family issues and I just clung to running as an escape. When I had mentioned to friends that things were a bit stressful, I had been praised for seeking refuge in running.

At the time it felt like the right thing to do. But there's only so far you can take it."

She realised that instead of confronting her worries, she had been craving the post-run high to drown them out. "I wasn't taking the time to talk about how I really felt and was sinking further and further into a dark place. I was punishing myself: somehow in the pain of everything that was going wrong, making myself feel worse made me feel better. I couldn't work out how to get rid of the pain, so in a self-destructive way making it worse felt really good. I had control again.

"While exercise provided some temporary relief it was not a substitute for professional mental health support," says Marianne. "Once I realised this I found that there were people who could help and support me. I didn't have to find the solutions on my own. There is no shame in needing help and once you can navigate the support systems, the experts out there can really change your life. We really need to be more aware of the warning signs of exercise addiction to help people get professional support to address the underlying issues.

"With the help of a brilliant team of health professionals (physio, psychologist and dietitian) I have learnt a lot about that self-destructive cycle and about my relationship with exercise. Although this peaked in the last year, some of it is deep-rooted so there have been no quick fixes. I have avoided a lot of questions I didn't want to answer but eventually found the courage to open up and talk about how I feel.

"I am not ready just yet to give up the dependency I have on exercise but I do make better decisions about it and I am more self-aware. I have to do this in my own time, this whole journey of recovery has to be at my pace and I will keep chipping away as best I can."

FURTHER READING

5k Move Your Way, Move Against Cancer website. Retrieved from https://5kyour way.org/

Aguiar, E. J., Morgan, P. J., Collins, C. E., Plotnikoff, R. C., & Callister, R. (2014). Efficacy of interventions that include diet, aerobic and resistance training components for type 2 diabetes prevention: A systematic review with meta-analysis. *International Journal of Behavioral Nutrition and Physical Activity*, 11(1), 2.

Anderson, L., Oldridge, N., Thompson, D. R., Zwisler, A. D., Rees, K., Martin, N., & Taylor, R. S. (2016). Exercise-based cardiac rehabilitation for coronary heart disease: Cochrane systematic review and meta-analysis. *Journal of the American College of Cardiology*, 67(1), 1–12.

Asthma Advice Sheets. Retrieved from www.asthma.org.uk/advice/living-with-asthma/exercise-and-activities/

Avery, L., Flynn, D., Van Wersch, A., Sniehotta, F. F., & Trenell, M. I. (2012). Changing physical activity behavior in type 2 diabetes: A systematic review and meta-analysis of behavioral interventions. *Diabetes Care*, 35(12), 2681–2689.

Barnett, I., van Sluijs, E. M., & Ogilvie, D. (2012). Physical activity and transitioning to retirement: A systematic review. *American Journal of Preventive Medicine*, 43(3), 329–336.

Baxter, S., Johnson, M., Payne, N., Buckley-Woods, H., Blank, L., Hock, E., . . . Goyder, E. (2016). Promoting and maintaining physical activity in the transition to retirement: A systematic review of interventions for adults around retirement age. *International Journal of Behavioral Nutrition and Physical Activity*, 13(1), 12.

Berczik, K., Szabó, A., Griffiths, M. D., Kurimay, T., Kun, B., Urbán, R., & Demetrovics, Z. (2012). Exercise addiction: Symptoms, diagnosis, epidemiology, and etiology. *Substance Use & Misuse*, 47(4), 403–417.

Biddle, S. J., Ciaccioni, S., Thomas, G., & Vergeer, I. (2019). Physical activity and mental health in children and adolescents: An updated review of reviews and an analysis of causality. *Psychology of Sport and Exercise*, 42, 146–155.

Biddle, S. J., & Nigg, C. R. (2000). Theories of exercise behavior. *International Journal of Sport Psychology*, 31(2), 290–304.

Bircher, J., Griffiths, M. D., Kasos, K., Demetrovics, Z., & Szabo, A. (2017). Exercise addiction and personality: A two-decade systematic review of the empirical literature (1995–2015). *Baltic Journal of Sports and Health Sciences*, 3(106), 19–33.

Burgess, E., Hassmén, P., Welvaert, M., & Pumpa, K. L. (2017). Behavioural treatment strategies improve adherence to lifestyle intervention programmes in adults with obesity: A systematic review and meta-analysis. *Clinical Obesity*, 7(2), 105–114.

Cancer Advice Sheet. Retrieved from www.cancerresearchuk.org/about-cancer/coping/physically/exercise-guidelines

Conn, V. S., Hafdahl, A. R., Porock, D. C., McDaniel, R., & Nielsen, P. J. (2006). A meta-analysis of exercise interventions among people treated for cancer. *Supportive Care in Cancer*, 14(7), 699–712.

Davis, C. L., Tomporowski, P. D., McDowell, J. E., Austin, B. P., Miller, P. H., Yanasak, N. E., . . . Naglieri, J. A. (2011). Exercise improves executive function and achievement and alters brain activation in overweight children: A randomized, controlled trial. *Health Psychology*, 30(1), 91.

Diabetes Advice Sheet. Retrieved from www.diabetes.co.uk/exercise-for-diabetics.html

Firth, J., Rosenbaum, S., Stubbs, B., Gorczynski, P., Yung, A. R., & Vancampfort, D. (2016). Motivating factors and barriers towards exercise in severe mental illness: A systematic review and meta-analysis. *Psychological Medicine*, 46(14), 2869–2881.

Football Fans in Training. Retrieved from https://ffit.org.uk/

Guthold, R., Stevens, G. A., Riley, L. M., & Bull, F. C. (2018). Worldwide trends in insufficient physical activity from 2001 to 2016: A pooled analysis of 358 population-based surveys with 1· 9 million participants. *The Lancet Global Health*, 6(10), e1077–e1086.

Guthold, R., Stevens, G. A., Riley, L. M., & Bull, F. C. (2020). Global trends in insufficient physical activity among adolescents: A pooled analysis of 298 population-based surveys with 1·6 million participants. *The Lancet Child & Adolescent Health*, 4(1), 23–35.

Hagger, M., Chatzisarantis, N., & Biddle, S. (2002). A meta-analytic review of the theories of reasoned action and planned behavior in physical activity: Predictive validity and the contribution of additional variables. *Journal of Sport & Exercise Psychology*, 24(1), 3–32.

Hausenblas, H. A., Carron, A. V., & Mack, D. E. (1997). Application of the theories of reasoned action and planned behavior to exercise behavior: A meta-analysis. *Journal of Sport and Exercise Psychology*, 19(1), 36–51.

Hausenblas, H. A., & Downs, D. S. (2002). Exercise dependence: A systematic review. *Psychology of Sport and Exercise*, 3(2), 89–123.

Heart disease and Activity Information Leaflet. Retrieved from www.bhf.org.uk/informationsupport/publications/being-active/understanding-physical-activity

Ingledew, D. K., Markland, D., & Medley, A. R. (1998). Exercise motives and stages of change. *Journal of Health Psychology*, 3(4), 477–489.

Josefsson, T., Lindwall, M., & Archer, T. (2014). Physical exercise intervention in depressive disorders: Meta-analysis and systematic review. *Scandinavian Journal of Medicine & Science in Sports*, 24(2), 259–272.

Lox, C. L., Ginis, K. A. M., & Petruzzello, S. J. (2016). *The psychology of exercise: Integrating theory and practice*. Abingdon, Oxon: Taylor & Francis.

McPhee, J. S., French, D. P., Jackson, D., Nazroo, J., Pendleton, N., & Degens, H. (2016). Physical activity in older age: Perspectives for healthy ageing and frailty. *Biogerontology*, 17(3), 567–580.

Mini Mermaids Running Club. Retrieved from www.minimermaiduk.com/

Morgan, F., Battersby, A., Weightman, A. L., Searchfield, L., Turley, R., Morgan, H., . . . Ellis, S. (2016). Adherence to exercise referral schemes by participants – what do providers and commissioners need to know? A systematic review of barriers and facilitators. *BMC Public Health*, 16(1), 227.

Ormel, H. L., van der Schoot, G. G. F., Sluiter, W. J., Jalving, M., Gietema, J. A., & Walenkamp, A. M. E. (2018). Predictors of adherence to exercise interventions during and after cancer treatment: A systematic review. *Psycho-oncology*, 27(3), 713–724.

Radovic, S., Gordon, M. S., & Melvin, G. A. (2017). Should we recommend exercise to adolescents with depressive symptoms? A meta-analysis. *Journal of Paediatrics and Child Health*, 53(3), 214–220.

Schreiber, K., & Hausenblas, H. A. (2015). *The truth about exercise addiction: Understanding the dark side of thinspiration*. Lanham, MD: Rowman & Littlefield.

Silverfit. Retrieved from www.silverfit.org.uk/

Skates Dagenham. Retrieved from www.connectsport.co.uk/skates-dagenham

Speck, R. M., Courneya, K. S., Mâsse, L. C., Duval, S., & Schmitz, K. H. (2010). An update of controlled physical activity trials in cancer survivors: A systematic review and meta-analysis. *Journal of Cancer Survivorship*, 4(2), 87–100.

Sporting Heads website. Retrieved from https://sportingheads.com/

Taylor, R. S., Brown, A., Ebrahim, S., Jolliffe, J., Noorani, H., Rees, K., . . . Oldridge, N. (2004). Exercise-based rehabilitation for patients with coronary heart disease: Systematic review and meta-analysis of randomized controlled trials. *The American Journal of Medicine*, 116(10), 682–692.

Tomporowski, P. D., Davis, C. L., Miller, P. H., & Naglieri, J. A. (2008). Exercise and children's intelligence, cognition, and academic achievement. *Educational Psychology Review*, 20(2), 111.

Vernberg, E. M., Hambrick, E. P., Cho, B., & Hendrickson, M. L. (2016). Positive psychology and disaster mental health: Strategies for working with children and adolescents. *Journal of Clinical Psychology*, 72(12), 1333–1347.

World Health Organisation Physical Activity Sheets. Retrieved from www.who.int/health-topics/physical-activity

REFERENCES

Ajzen, I. (1991). The theory of planned behaviour. *Organizational Behavior and Human Decision Processes*, 50, 179–211.

Alharbi, M., Gallagher, R., Neubeck, L., Bauman, A., Prebill, G., Kirkness, A., & Randall, S. (2017). Exercise barriers and the relationship to self-efficacy for exercise over 12 months of a lifestyle-change program for people with heart disease and/or diabetes. *European Journal of Cardiovascular Nursing*, 16(4), 309–317.

Ali, S., Stone, M. A., Peters, J. L., Davies, M. J., & Khunti, K. (2006). The prevalence of co-morbid depression in adults with Type 2 diabetes: A systematic review and meta-analysis. *Diabetic Medicine*, 23(11), 1165–1173.

Baker, I. D. I. (2012). *Diabetes: The silent pandemic and its impact on Australia.* Melbourne: Baker IDI.

Bandura, A. (1989). Human agency in social cognitive theory. *American Psychologist*, 44(9), 1175.

Bandura, A. (1997). *Self-efficacy: The exercise of control.* New York: W. H. Freeman.

Barlow, S. E. (2007). Expert committee recommendations regarding the prevention, assessment, and treatment of child and adolescent overweight and obesity: Summary report. *Pediatrics*, 120(4), S164–S192.

Bender, B. G., Milgrom, H., & Apter, A. (2003). Adherence intervention research: What have we learned and what do we do next? *Journal of Allergy and Clinical Immunology*, 112, 489–494.

Blumenthal, J. A., Sherwood, A., Rogers, S. D., Babyak, M. A., Murali Doraiswamy, P., Watkins, L., . . . Waugh, R. (2007). Understanding prognostic benefits of exercise and antidepressant therapy for persons with depression and heart disease: The UPBEAT study – rationale, design, and methodological issues. *Clinical Trials*, 4(5), 548–559.

Braman, S. S. (2006). The global burden of asthma. *Chest*, 130, 4S–12S.

Bratland-Sanda, S., Martinsen, E. W., Rosenvinge, J. H., Rø, Ø., Hoffart, A., & Sundgot-Borgen, J. (2011). Exercise dependence score in patients with longstanding eating disorders and controls: The importance of affect regulation and physical activity intensity. *European Eating Disorders Review*, 19(3), 249–255.

Bryan, A. D., Magnan, R. E., Nilsson, R., Marcus, B. H., Tompkins, S. A., & Hutchison, K. E. (2011). The big picture of individual differences in physical activity behavior change: A transdisciplinary approach. *Psychology of Sport and Exercise*, 12, 20–26.

Burton, E., Farrier, K., Lewin, G., Pettigrew, S., Hill, A. M., Airey, P., . . . Hill, K. D. (2017). Motivators and barriers for older people participating in resistance training: A systematic review. *Journal of Aging and Physical Activity*, 25(2), 311–324.

Burton, N. W., Khan, A., & Brown, W. J. (2012). How, where and with whom? Physical activity context preferences of three adult groups at risk of inactivity. *British Journal of Sports Medicine*, 46(16), 1125–1131.

Callaghan, P., Khalil, E., Morres, I., & Carter, T. (2011). Pragmatic randomised controlled trial of preferred intensity exercise in women living with depression. *BMC Public Health*, 11, 465.

Caserta, M. S., & Gillett, P. A. (1998). Older women's feelings about exercise and their adherence to an aerobic regimen over time. *Gerontologist*, 38(5), 602–609.

Centers for Disease Control and Prevention (2018). *Diabetes*. Retrieved from www.cdc.gov/nchs/data/hus/2018/014.pdf

Clark, N. M., Gong, M., & Kaciroti, N. (2001). A model of self-regulation for control of chronic disease. *Health Education & Behavior*, 28(6), 769–782.

Dalle Grave, R., Calugi, S., & Marchesini, G. (2008). Compulsive exercise to control shape or weight in eating disorders: Prevalence, associated features, and treatment outcome. *Comprehensive Psychiatry*, 49(4), 346–352.

Davis, C. L., Tomporowski, P. D., McDowell, J. E., Austin, B. P., Miller, P. H., Yanasak, N. E., . . . Naglieri, J. A. (2011). Exercise improves executive function and achievement and alters brain activation in overweight children: A randomized, controlled trial. *Health Psychology*, 30(1), 91.

Davis, K. J., Disantostefano, R., & Peden, D. B. (2011). Is Johnny wheezing? Parent – child agreement in the childhood asthma in America survey. *Pediatric Allergy and Immunology*, 22(1), 31–35.

Deci, E. L., & Ryan, R. M. (1985). *Intrinsic motivation and self-determination in human behavior* (1st ed.). New York: Plenum Press.

Deci, E. L., & Ryan, R. M. (2000). The "what" and "why" of goal pursuits: Human needs and the self-determination of behavior. *Psychological Inquiry*, 11(4), 227–268.

Ding, D., Lawson, K. D., Kolbe-Alexander, T. L., Finkelstein, E. A., Katzmarzyk, P. T., Van Mechelen, W., . . . Lancet Physical Activity Series 2 Executive Committee. (2016). The economic burden of physical inactivity: A global analysis of major non-communicable diseases. *The Lancet*, 388(10051), 1311–1324.

Dishman, R., Motl, R. W., Sallis, J. F., Dunn, A. L., Birnbaum, A. S., Welk, G. J., . . . Jobe, J. B. (2005). Self-management strategies mediate self-efficacy and physical activity. *American Journal of Preventive Medicine*, 29(1), 10–18.

Eccles, J. S., & Harold, R. D. (1991). Gender differences in sport involvement: Applying the Eccles' expectancy-value model. *Journal of Applied Sport Psychology*, 3(1), 7–35.

Egorov, A. Y., & Szabo, A. (2013). The exercise paradox: An interactional model for a clearer conceptualization of exercise addiction. *Journal of Behavioral Addictions*, 2(4), 199–208.

Elavsky, S. (2010). Longitudinal examination of the exercise and self-esteem model in middle-aged women. *Journal of Sport and Exercise Psychology*, 32(6), 862–880.

Elkins, W. L., Cohen, D. A., Koralewicz, L. M., & Taylor, S. N. (2004). After school activities, overweight, and obesity among inner city youth. *Journal of Adolescence*, 27(2), 181–189.

Ellis, A. (1957). Rational psychotherapy and individual psychology. *Journal of Individual Psychology*, 13, 38–44.

Farooq, M. A., Parkinson, K. N., Adamson, A. J., Pearce, M. S., Reilly, J. K., Hughes, A. R., . . . Reilly, J. J. (2018). Timing of the decline in physical activity in childhood and adolescence: Gateshead millennium cohort study. *British Journal of Sports Medicine*, 52(15), 1002–1006.

Ferrand, C., Nasarre, S., Hautier, C., & Bonnefoy, M. (2012). Aging and well-being in French older adults regularly practicing physical activity: A self-determination perspective. *Journal of Aging and Physical Activity*, 20(2), 215–230.

Festinger, L. (1954). A theory of social comparison processes. *Human Relations*, 7(2), 117–140.

Fishbein, M., & Ajzen, I. (1975). *Belief attitude, intention and behavior. An introduction to theory and research*. Reading, MA: Addison-Wesley.

Fredricks, J. A., & Eccles, J. S. (2005). Family socialization, gender, and sport motivation and involvement. *Journal of Sport and Exercise Psychology*, 27(1), 3–31.

Fredrickson, B. L. (2004). The broaden – and – build theory of positive emotions. *Philosophical Transactions of the Royal Society of London. Series B: Biological Sciences*, 359(1449), 1367–1377.

Fredrickson, B. L., & Roberts, T. A. (1997). Objectification theory: Toward understanding women's lived experiences and mental health risks. *Psychology of Women Quarterly*, 21(2), 173–206.

Galvão, D. A., Newton, R. U., Gardiner, R. A., Girgis, A., Lepore, S. J., Stiller, A., . . . Chambers, S. K. (2015). Compliance to exercise-oncology guidelines in prostate cancer survivors and associations with psychological distress, unmet supportive care needs, and quality of life. *Psycho-Oncology*, 24(10), 1241–1249.

GBD Collaborators (2017). Global, regional and national incidence, prevalence and years lived with disability for 354 diseases and injuries for 195 countries and territories, 1990–2017; a systematic analysis for the Global Burden of Disease Study 2017. *The Lancet*, 392(10159), 1789–1858.

Grigsby, A. B., Anderson, R. J., Freedland, K. E., Clouse, R. E., & Lustman, P. J. (2002). Prevalence of anxiety in adults with diabetes: A systematic review. *Journal of Psychosomatic Research*, 53(6), 1053–1060.

Grimm, E. K., Swartz, A. M., Hart, T., Miller, N. E., & Strath, S. J. (2012). Comparison of the IPAQ-Short Form and accelerometery predictions of physical activity in older adults. *Journal of Aging and Physical Activity*, 20(1), 64–79.

Guthold, R., Stevens, G. A., Riley, L. M., & Bull, F. C. (2020). Global trends in insufficient physical activity among adolescents: A pooled analysis of 298 population-based surveys with 1·6 million participants. *The Lancet Child & Adolescent Health*, 4(1), 23–35.

Hakola, L., Hassinen, M., Komulainen, P., Lakka, T. A., Savonen, K., & Rauramaa, R. (2015). Correlates of low physical activity levels in aging men and women: The DR's EXTRA Study (ISRCTN45977199). *Journal of Aging and Physical Activity, 23*(2), 247–255.

Hallal, P. C., Andersen, L. B., Bull, F. C., Guthold, R., Haskell, W., Ekelund, U., & Lancet Physical Activity Series Working Group. (2012). Global physical activity levels: Surveillance progress, pitfalls, and prospects. *The Lancet, 380*(9838), 247–257.

Harvey, J. A., Chastin, S. F. M., & Skelton, D. A. (2015). How sedentary are older people? A systematic review of the amount of sedentary behavior. *Journal of Aging and Physical Activity, 23*(3), 471–487.

Harvey, S. B., Øverland, S., Hatch, S. L., Wessely, S., Mykletun, A., & Hotopf, M. (2018). Exercise and the prevention of depression: Results of the HUNT cohort study. *American Journal of Psychiatry, 175*(1), 28–36.

Huppertz, C., Bartels, M., Jansen, I. E., Boomsma, D. I., Willemsen, G., de Moor, M. H., & de Geus, E. J. (2014). A twin-sibling study on the relationship between exercise attitudes and exercise behavior. *Behavior Genetics, 44*(1), 45–55.

Huy, C., Schneider, S., & Thiel, A. (2010). Perceptions of aging and health behavior: Determinants of a healthy diet in an older german population. *The Journal of Nutrition, Health & Aging, 14*(5), 381–385.

Ibrahim, E. M., & Al-Homaidh, A. (2011). Physical activity and survival after breast cancer diagnosis: Meta-analysis of published studies. *Medical Oncology, 28*(3), 753–765.

Jessor, R., & Jessor, S. L. (1977). *Problem behavior and psychosocial development: A longitudinal study of youth.* New York: Academic Press.

Kahn, E. B., Ramsey, L. T., Brownson, R. C., et al., (2002). The effectiveness of interventions to increase physical activity: A systematic review. *American Journal of Preventive Medicine, 22*(4), 73–107.

Kandola, A., Lewis, G., Osborn, D. P., Stubbs, B., & Hayes, J. F. (2020). Depressive symptoms and objectively measured physical activity and sedentary behaviour throughout adolescence: A prospective cohort study. *The Lancet Psychiatry, 7*(3), 262–271.

Kenfield, S. A., Stampfer, M. J., Giovannucci, E., & Chan, J. M. (2011). Physical activity and survival after prostate cancer diagnosis in the health professionals follow-up study. *Journal of Clinical Oncology, 29*(6), 726.

Kolt, G. S., Driver, R. P., & Giles, L. C. (2004). Why older Australians participate in exercise and sport. *Journal of Aging and Physical Activity, 12*(2), 185–198.

Kostanski, M., & Gullone, E. (1998). Adolescent body image dissatisfaction: Relationships with self-esteem, anxiety, and depression controlling for body mass. *The Journal of Child Psychology and Psychiatry and Allied Disciplines*, 39(2), 255–262.

Krowchuk, D. P., Kreiter, S. R., Woods, C. R., Sinal, S. H., & DuRant, R. H. (1998). Problem dieting behaviors among young adolescents. *Archives of Pediatrics & Adolescent Medicine*, 152(9), 884–888.

Lenfant, C., & Hurd, S. S. (1990). National asthma education program. *Chest*, 98(1), 226–227.

Levy, B. (2009). Stereotypes embodiment: A psychosocial approach to aging. *Current Directions in Psychological Science*, 18, 332–336.

Mallol, J., Crane, J., Mutius, E., Odhiambo, J., Keil, U., & Stewart, A. (2013). The international study of asthma and allergies in childhood (ISAAC) phase three: A global synthesis. *Allergologia et Immunopathologia*, 41(2), 73–85.

McAuley, E., Lox, C., & Duncan, T. (1993). Long-term maintenance of exercise, self-efficacy, and physiological change in older adults. *Journal of Gerontology*, 48(4), 218–224.

McAuley, E., Shaffer, S. M., & Rudolph, D. (1995). Affective responses to acute exercise in elderly impaired males: The moderating effects of self-efficacy and age. *The International Journal of Aging and Human Development*, 41(1), 13–27.

McFadden, E. R., Jr., & Gilbert, I. A. (1994). Exercise-induced asthma. *New England Journal of Medicine*, 330(19), 1362–1367.

Michie, S., Johnston, M., Abraham, C., Lawton, R., Parker, D., & Walker, A. (2005). Making psychological theory useful for implementing evidence based practice: A consensus approach. *BMJ Quality & Safety*, 14(1), 26–33.

Mónok, K., Berczik, K., Urbán, R., Szabo, A., Griffiths, M. D., Farkas, J., et al. (2012). Psychometric properties and concurrent validity of two exercise addiction measures: A population wide study. *Psychology of Sport and Exercise*, 13(6), 739–746.

Moore, L. L., Lombardi, D. A., White, M. J., Campbell, J. L., Oliveria, S. A., & Ellison, R. C. (1991). Influence of parents' physical activity levels on activity levels of young children. *The Journal of Paediatrics*, 118(2), 215–219.

Nader, P. R., Bradley, R. H., Houts, R. M., McRitchie, S. L., & O'Brien, M. (2008). Moderate-to-vigorous physical activity from ages 9 to 15 years. *Jama*, 300(3), 295–305.

Ogden, C. L., Carroll, M. D., & Flegal, K. M. (2008). High body mass index for age among US children and adolescents, 2003–2006. *Journal of the American Medical Association*, 299, 2401–2405.

Outar, L., Turner, M. J., Wood, A. G., & Lowry, R. (2018). "I need to go to the gym": Exploring the use of rational emotive behaviour therapy upon exercise addiction, irrational and rational beliefs. *Performance Enhancement & Health, 6*(2), 82–93.

Parsons, J. E., Adler, T. F., Futterman, R., Goff, S. B., Kaczala, C. M., Meece, J. L., & Midgley, C. (1983). Expectancies, values, and academic behaviors. *Achievement and Achievement Motives, 75*–146.

Pate, R. R., Pfeiffer, K A., Trost, S. G., Ziegler, P., & Dowda, M. (2004). Physical activity among children attending preschools. *Paediatrics, 114,* 1258–1263.

Pedisic, Z., Shrestha, N., Kovalchik, S., Stamatakis, E., Liangruenrom, N., Grgic, J., . . . Oja, P. (2019). Is running associated with a lower risk of all-cause, cardiovascular and cancer mortality, and is the more the better? A systematic review and meta-analysis. *British Journal of Sports Medicine.*

Perry, J. (2018). *Ultra-endurance athletes and their use of fitness technologies: Filling a social void or fuelling an exercise addiction?* Retrieved from https://performanceinmind. files.wordpress.com/2018/08/exercise-addiction-summary-perry.pdf

Prochaska, J., & DiClemente, C. C. (1983). Stages and processes of self-change of smoking: Toward an integrative model of change. *Journal of Consulting and Clinical Psychology, 51,* 390–395.

Pyky, R., Koivumaa-Honkanen, H., Leinonen, A. M., Ahola, R., Hirvonen, N., Enwald, H., . . . Mäntysaari, M. (2017). Effect of tailored, gamified, mobile physical activity intervention on life satisfaction and self-rated health in young adolescent men: A population-based, randomized controlled trial (MOPO study). *Computers in Human Behavior, 72,* 13–22.

Rush, A. J., Trivedi, M. H., Wisniewski, S. R., Nierenberg, A. A., Stewart, J. W., Warden, D., . . . McGrath, P. J. (2006). Acute and longer-term outcomes in depressed outpatients requiring one or several treatment steps: A STAR* D report. *American Journal of Psychiatry, 163*(11), 1905–1917.

Scheer, V., & Hahn, S. (2014). *Conference paper: Are ultramarathon runners exercise addicts?* German Association of Sports Medicine; 45th Sports Medicine Congress September 2014.

Scheerder, J., Thomis, M., Vanreusel, B., Lefevre, J., Renson, R., Vanden Eynde, B., & Beunen, G. P. (2006). Sports participation among females from adolescence to adulthood: A longitudinal study. *International Review for the Sociology of Sport, 41*(3–4), 413–430.

Schmidt, M., Egger, F., & Conzelmann, A. (2015). Delayed positive effects of an acute bout of coordinative exercise on children's attention. *Perceptual and Motor Skills, 121*(2), 431–446.

Schwarzer, R. (2008). Modelling health behaviour change: How to predict and modify the adoption and maintenance of health behaviours. *Applied Psychology*, 57(1), 1–29.

Sicilia, A., Alias-Garcia, A., Ferriz, R., & Moreno-Murcia, J. A. (2013). Spanish adaptation and validation of the Exercise Addiction Inventory (EAI). *Psicothema*, 25(3), 377–383.

Skinner, B. F. (1989). *The origins of cognitive though. Recent issues in the analysis of behavior.* Columbus, OH: Merrill Publishing Company.

Slater, A., & Tiggemann, M. (2011). Gender differences in adolescent sport participation, teasing, self-objectification and body image concerns. *Journal of Adolescence*, 34(3), 455–463.

Sonstroem, R. J., & Morgan, W. P. (1989). Exercise and self-esteem: Rationale and model. *Medicine & Science in Sports & Exercise*, 21(3), 329–337.

Szabo, A., & Griffiths, M. D. (2007). Exercise addiction in british sport science students. *International Journal of Mental Health and Addiction*, 5(1), 25–28.

Tammelin, T., Näyhä, S., Laitinen, J., Rintamäki, H., & Järvelin, M. R. (2003). Physical activity and social status in adolescence as predictors of physical inactivity in adulthood. *Preventive Medicine*, 37(4), 375–381.

Telama, R., Yang, X., Hirvensalo, M., & Raitakari, O. (2006). Participation in organized youth sport as a predictor of adult physical activity: A 21-year longitudinal study. *Paediatric Exercise Science*, 18(1), 76–88.

Tremblay, M. S., Inman, J. W., & Willms, J. D. (2000). The relationship between physical activity, self-esteem, and academic achievement in 12-year-old children. *Paediatric Exercise Science*, 12(3), 312–323.

Trott, M., Jackson, S. E., Firth, J., Jacob, L., Grabovac, I., Mistry, A., . . . Smith, L. (2020). A comparative meta-analysis of the prevalence of exercise addiction in adults with and without indicated eating disorders. *Eating and Weight Disorders-Studies on Anorexia, Bulimia and Obesity*, 1–10.

Wang, H., Naghavi, M., Allen, C., Barber, R. M., Bhutta, Z. A., Carter, A., . . . Coggeshall, M. (2016). Global, regional, and national life expectancy, all-cause mortality, and cause-specific mortality for 249 causes of death, 1980–2015: A systematic analysis for the global burden of disease study 2015. *The Lancet*, 388(10053), 1459–1544.

Warner, R., & Griffiths, M. D. (2006). A qualitative thematic analysis of exercise addiction: An exploratory study. *International Journal of Mental Health and Addiction*, 4, 13–26.

Watts, R. W., McLennan, G., Bassham, I., & El-Saadi, O. (1997). Do patients with asthma fill their prescriptions? A primary compliance study. *Australian Family Physician*, 26(1), 4–6.

Wilcox, S., King, A. C., Brassington, G. S., & Ahn, D. K. (1999). Physical activity preferences of middle-aged and older adults: A community analysis. *Journal of Aging and Physical Activity*, 7(4), 386–399.

Williams, B., Hoskins, G., Pow, J., Neville, R., Mukhopadhyay, S., & Coyle, J. (2010). Low exercise among children with asthma: A culture of over protection? *British Journal of General Practice*, 60, 319–326.

Williamson, D., Dewey, A., & Steinberg, H. (2001). Mood change through physical exercise in nine-to ten-year-old children. *Perceptual and Motor Skills*, 93(1), 311–316.

Wolinsky, F. D., Stump, T. E., & Clark, D. O. (1995). Antecedents and consequences of physical activity and exercise among older adults. *The Gerontologist*, 35(4), 451–462.

World Health Organisation (2018a). *Fact sheet on diabetes*. Retrieved from www.who.int/news-room/fact-sheets/detail/diabetes

World Health Organisation (2018b). *Fact sheet on physical activity*. Retrieved from www.who.int/news-room/fact-sheets/detail/physical-activity

Youngman, J., & Simpson, D. (2014). Risk for exercise addiction: A comparison of triathletes training for Sprint-, Olympic-, Half-Ironman-, and Ironman-Distance triathlons. *Journal of Clinical Sport Psychology*, 8, 19–37.